The Millionaire
Method

How to get out of Debt and Earn Financial Freedom by Understanding the Psychology of the Millionaire Mind

R.L. Adams

R.L. ADAMS

This Page Intentionally Left Blank

From The

Inspirational Books Series

by

R.L. Adams

All Rights Reserved

Legal Notices

This Page Intentionally Left Blank

CONTENTS

PROLOGUE

"When I was young I thought that money was the most important thing in life; now that I am old I know that it is." – Oscar Wilde

In the hearts of men and women all across the face of this earth, there exists a dream. It's a dream that's harbored by so many, but fulfilled by so few. It's a dream that includes money, wealth, and financial freedom – words that have become synonymous with modern economies. It's a dream filled with visions of grandeur, far off destinations, and a life of leisure. But, the dream is more than just about having lots of money. The dream held by so many across the globe, is about true freedom. It's about the freedom to go wherever you want, whenever you want, do whatever you want, and be with whomever you want. It's the freedom to not have to open your eyes in the morning, only to dread another day, while miserably treading through a life sucking nine-to-five job. It's the dream to be able to spend time with your loved ones, donate to your favorite charities, and focus on your spirituality. It's the dream to have complete freedom from daily responsibility and obligation.

But, how difficult is it to fulfill this dream? How much effort does it truly take to make it a reality? What does it take in order to have the freedom and wealth to untether the financial cord, and stop slaving away every moment of every day, just to get by? And, how is that some people are so seemingly good at achieving financial freedom, while others seem to fall further and further behind with each passing day? Around the world, people desire to learn the answers to these questions. They desire to fulfill the dream that burns like a roaring fire in their hearts. They desire to create a better life for themselves and the ones that they love. However, this dream, which exists in the eager-hearted men and women in the towns, cities, states, and countries of the world, is a seemingly insurmountable one. It's difficult beyond belief to live a life according to one's own rules. It's seemingly impossible to achieve, but the dream still lives on.

It's no secret that in today's burgeoning global economy, money makes the world go round, and those that hold the answers to the secrets of success are like the gatekeepers to the land of milk and honey. Because, ever since the dawn of modern society, money has punctured every element of our existence, yet the attainment of money has always evaded so many; the dream has slipped away all too often. So many people have strived for the dream of financial freedom, only to have life's many obligations and distractions, hinder and impede them in their vicious struggle to get ahead and stay there. Most falter, and because of it, the disparity between the rich, and the poor grows greater by the minute. The dream slips further and further away as people realize the immensity of the undertaking required to fulfill their life-long desires for true financial freedom.

However, this isn't the case for all. Some people are able to master their financial intelligence, and fulfill their life long dreams of financial freedom. They go from allowing money to control them, to having complete and utter control over their financial destinies. They go from fearing and hating it, to respecting and nurturing it. They learn to understand money, and how their behavior affects their own bottom line. And, depending upon your own personal experiences and behavior when it comes to money, it's taken on a certain meaning for you as well. It evokes a certain emotional response, and elicits a certain set of feelings, when you hear those words.

For some, the mere thought of money creates feelings of fear and anxiety, while for others the same thoughts evoke happiness and elation. But, no matter how money makes you feel, having enough money to survive is a requirement for all people. Everyone knows that they need to have enough money to support themselves financially, whatever that base level of support may be. This involves having enough money to meet the basic human needs for food, shelter, and the other necessities in life. For others, having enough means keeping up with and supporting their financial lifestyles that are fraught with debt and expense. Yet, to even others, money is something far different. Having enough money to survive isn't merely enough for them. They want to make enough money to thrive.

To these, individuals who have taken to understand money, they devote their lives to thriving, and not just surviving. They build up their wealth, just as a general would build up his army in an effort to wage a war to earn more income. Their money becomes like soldiers that make more money, and in turn, they're able to accumulate excessive amounts of wealth, and create vast fortunes by putting every dollar they have to work. They're able to put their money to work, even as they sleep, allowing it to grow, foster, and blossom into more money. They understand money. They understand just what power it has on people, and how it affects their behavior. But, they learn to control it. They learn to control and manipulate money to serve them, not defeat them.

The uncanny ability for the seldom few to amass these great fortunes, further creates a mystique around money. To the rest of the world, these men and women are the elusive pinnacles of success. They are the captains of industry and the subject of widespread rumors, but more importantly, they are the individuals who persevered and achieved vast amounts of success in the face of great adversity. They have the money and wealth to do what they want, when they want, and with whom they want to. But, it wasn't always that way for them. Just like everyone else, they struggled through the difficult times, and pushed through; they never gave up. They never gave up on their desire to achieve wealth, and live a life of abundance. They delayed their gratification for pleasure, methodically invested, and carefully plotted their way along the road to success.

Mainstream media has a tendency to elevate those who have achieved these kinds of notable monetary successes in life, since so many individuals across the globe envy them. They are the financially free. They are the world's upper class – the millionaires and the billionaires. But, all too often, we become disenchanted by the wealthy. We look at them with scorn and doubt, questioning their tactics, and undermining their principles. How did they achieve such great success? Surely, they had to step on many toes along the way, or betray scores of people on their quest to success, right? But, the truth of the matter is that they adhered to a set of rules and guidelines, which aided them along their pathway to great success. And, when they faltered, they corrected it, constantly assessing and reassessing their progress until they reached their goals. Eventually, they persevered.

But, it's very natural to want to look at the rich and wealthy with disdain. After all, they've achieved notable successes while the vast majority of people wallow away, slaving in their nine-to-five jobs, while struggling to balance families and social lives. The rich live abundant and carefree lifestyles, while the poor rot away in misery and despair. But, the biggest and most important elements that people don't see is, how much failure and defeat those that succeeded in life suffered before they achieved great success. They don't see the heartaches, the sleepless nights, or the desperate pleas they had to endure to get to where they are today. They only see the end result; they only see the current lifestyles as mainstream media portrays them.

This portrayal by the media fascinates the world. It fascinates them in a way that either disgusts them or attracts them. But, this isn't something new – the fascination with the rich starts at a very early age. When we're but children in school, we learn to elevate the seldom few who are born into lives of wealth. The rich become popular in school, well known in social circles, and are extended favors from an economic system where like-minded opportunists believe in rewarding one another for the achievements of their successes. In effect, the rich seem to get richer, and the poor continue to wallow in debt. And, straddled with this debt, most of the world's population goes through the motions of life, while attempting to hold onto their elusive desires of becoming rich. They watch the lives of the rich and famous with wide eyes as they gallivant across the globe in a seemingly endless spree of spending and pleasure-driven pursuits. Popularized by mainstream media, these lifestyles evade nearly every aspect of our lives. We see and hear it on television, in the magazines, on the radio, and on the Internet. From a very young age, we then begin to worship money in a seemingly endless chase towards its attainment.

However, the stark realities that exist in our consumer-driven society are that it's specifically designed and structured to hold us back from attaining financial freedom. From the moment we step foot into a higher education university, through every other day in our lives, we are straddled with the offers for credit. Our hunger and our thirst to spend and enjoy life, beckons us to push beyond our financial means. Even when we don't have the money to support our desires, countless companies are willing to help support our debt habits. They're willing to help us lease that new car, buy that new entertainment system, or go on that luxury vacation. Offers stream through by email, snail mail, telephone, magazines, newspapers, and televisions. Inundated and bombarded by these offers, the temptations to spend mounts, and they seem to exist at every turn and corner.

Although the majority of the world's populations now live in democratic economies, the unfortunate truth is that the majority of people will never get ahead. The bulk of the world's population will never amass a fortune sizable enough to put them on easy street, so to speak, because of a system that's designed to play into people's basal impulses. Around every corner, there exists a creditor just waiting to help us gain pleasure by increasing our access to money. But, the dream to succeed in life still stays alive. The burning desire to get ahead doesn't die, even when people understand the odds are seemingly stacked up against them. So, what does it really take then to make progress in the world? How do you move from the bottom of the rung to the top of the ladder while avoiding the temptations that exist around every corner?

These questions have plagued people for a long time. And, if you've been frustrated in trying to get ahead in life, you're not alone. You're not alone in your pursuit to want a better life for yourself and for your family. You're not alone in your secret desires for money, wealth, and prestige. However, the traps exist all around you. The traps that suck people in, and divert their attention are plentiful. They are life's distractions that are waiting to hook you, and drag you down. They're everywhere you turn, and no matter where you are, they exist all around you.

So, how do you escape this rat race called life? How do you extricate yourself from the shackles of debt? How do you move up in life when everything seems to be dragging you down? Well, the purpose of this book is to help answer these questions. The purpose of this book is to guide you through the principles of success, principles that you must adhere to in order to get ahead in life. These principles aren't brand new, but the approach to understanding them is. If you come with me on this journey, I'll help to open your eyes to a world that exists right in front of your face, but that's nearly impossible to see. It's a world where you can begin to see things for what they really are, and embark on the road to understanding your behavior, stop the bleeding of debt and expenses, and create real lasting wealth.

But, the problem is that, most of the world's corporations don't want you to be educated on success principles. They don't want you to understand the psychology that pushes you to purchase their goods or engage their services. Because, when a person truly understands himself or herself, and the psychologies behind succeeding in life, they won't be as susceptible to throwing their money away at the various distractions that life tends to offer them. However, coming to these realizations and making lasting improvements towards change in your life, are going to be difficult. It's going to be difficult to break patterns that you've become accustomed to. It's going to be difficult to push through your present day limitations without a great amount of pressure and effort on your part.

If you're willing to understand just what it takes to succeed in life, and are willing to do the work to change your lifestyle to adapt to the principles of success, over time, you will succeed. But, it's about more than just monetary success. It's about more than just currency in the bank. It's about living a balanced life, one where your emotional, spiritual, mental, physical, and financial realms align. It's about living a happy and fulfilled life that's tempered with balance, rather than fraught with extremes. If you're ready to embark on this journey, and you're tired of living the same life that's lead you to where you are today, then come with me on this voyage of financial achievement, and learn the millionaire method.

1
THE MILLIONAIRE METHOD

"Formal education will make you a living; self-education will make you a fortune." – Jim Rohn

Jake Harris opened his eyes at 5 o'clock in the morning, just as he had done for the past twenty-five years he had been in business for himself. He no longer needed an alarm clock in order to get out of bed. He had conditioned himself to wake naturally at that time over the course of decades of hard work. And, although he no longer needed to head into work so early in the day, he still did. He did it because he cared enough about his business to go in early. Jake was a man very attentive to details. He would calculate, judge, interpret, and conceive of all the various tasks required to get him from one point to the next, while steadily growing his business.

He rolled out of bed to greet the new day, and tackle another list of items he had to do. As a business owner, he always had the responsibility of running his business in the back of his mind. However, Jake Harris wasn't just your ordinary business owner. At the age of thirty-five he went into business for himself after purchasing a junkyard in rural Texas, just outside the city limits of Dallas. He had done his research in determining the need for spare truck and car parts in the area. Every single day, he went into work to greet his employees and help his customers find the parts that they needed. Every single day he carefully tracked and followed the numbers, expanding and growing his business at every opportunity he could take.

He walked into the bathroom to wash his face while his wife still lay asleep in bed. Their two children had already gone off to college to attend some of the finest universities in the country. He looked at his face in the mirror as he prepared himself for another day at work. He breathed in the clean air into his lungs, and ran his hand through his dark thick hair. Today was an important day for Jake Harris. Today was the day he would sit down for a national money magazine interview that wanted to chronicle his journey from a ward of the state as a child, to one of the wealthiest people in Texas. It almost didn't feel real. His journey and climb to the top was strife with disappointments along the way. There were many times along his journey when he just wanted to throw his hands up in the air in silent resignation, but he kept pushing through.

He thought back to his days as a youth and remembered how eager he was about life. He remembered how much he wanted to prove a point to himself and everyone else around him. He wanted to prove that he could succeed. He knew that he could do it. He knew that it was just a matter of time until he was able to break the mold and succeed. But, it didn't happen overnight. It didn't happen quickly at all, but he was methodical about it. He worked and toiled away, carefully planning and executing every minutia in great detail. There were so many lessons learned along the way, and so many things he would have wanted to do differently. But, he kept modifying his approach. He kept learning, growing stronger, and wiser. Now, he had something real and tangible to show for it. He had something he could be truly proud of now.

Jake jumped into his late model pickup truck and headed down to the yard that morning just as the sun was rising from its resting spot behind the grassy hills. He heard the roaring sputter of the engine as he made his way along the small town road that connected his home to his place of work. It was only a twenty-minute drive to the yard, and it was going to be a busy day. He parked, walked in, and stepped into his office. There was nothing special about Jake's office, nor was there anything special about the way in which he dressed or in the truck that he drove. No, Jake was a simple man. He never wanted to try to stand out from the rest of his employees or other people in any way.

Instead of buying a fancy car or truck, Jake invested his money into building up his yard. He poured countless dollars into tracking and analyzing the yard's inventory, and setting up a software system that could help customers find the parts they were looking for faster than ever before. He was all about efficiency. He worked to revolutionize the business, and in turn, his sales and his profits soared.

Jake sat down at his desk and powered on the computer screen. He ran through his daily task of items to do while he thought about the interview he had to prepare for in the next few hours. The thought of talking about his success intimidated him. It did so because he never wanted to appear as if he was bragging or boasting. He didn't want to alienate the people that he knew, who may read the article in the national magazine. It was a strange feeling, but Jake had agreed to it after a very steady behest from the editor.

The writer walked into the yard at 10 o'clock in the morning, just as he had scheduled to do so. When he arrived, he asked for the CEO's office and people gave him a strange look. They gave him a strange look because the employees of the yard didn't know Jake Harris as the CEO or the President of the company. They simply referred to him as Old Jake. When the writer realized this, he asked for Jake by his full name, and got a much more welcoming reception.

"Yeah, Old Jake? He's that way," an employee said, pointing in a direction of offices that meandered around a bend. The writer made his way through the long maze of corridors and offices, but couldn't find Jake's office in the cluster of offices. There was nothing special about Jake's office. No nametag, no sign that said "President & CEO," nothing like that. Eventually, the writer had to ask several more people where the office was, and had to knock on a few doors until he found Jake.

"Hi," he said to Jake.

"Hi there." Jake stood up to greet him. He sat behind a simple wood desk in simple non-descript office that looked out over the yard. Hundreds of books lined the bookshelves of the office.

"Jake Harris?"

"Yes."

"Oh, okay. It's nice to meet you. I'm Robert."

"Nice to meet you, Robert. Please have a seat. You look a little surprised?" Jake said.

"Yes, I guess I was expecting... something different."

"Different?" asked Jake.

"Yes, maybe that's not the right word."

Jake smiled. He knew exactly what Robert was talking about, but Jake never cared for a fancy office. He never cared for something that was going to set him apart from his employees. He didn't feel like he was above them, so he didn't act like it. He didn't treat them as if they worked for him, but rather, he treated them like family. That was how he thought every business should operate. It was about the people, and the relationships with those people. "I understand," he said in response.

"I hope I haven't offended you in any way," said Robert.

"No, of course you haven't." Jake smiled again.

"Okay," said Robert. He sat down in the simple chair in front of the desk and pulled out a notepad full of questions. "Do you mind if I record the conversation?" he asked, placing a small recording device on top of the desk.

"Not at all."

"Great, shall we get started then?"

"Sure."

"Mr. Harris, you seem like a pretty happy man," he said.

"Please call me Jake."

"Okay, Jake," he said. "I guess I'm just used to the formalities."

Jake sat back in his chair to think about the question before responding. "Well, I guess you could say that I'm doing what I love. This company is my baby, and I wouldn't trade it for the world."

"Can you tell me a little bit about how you got started?"

"Well, it's been twenty five years now. I won't sit here and lie to you that the road has been easy, but it certainly has been fulfilling. I never thought about turning this into the success that it is today; I just focused on the basics. I wanted to provide good value that was of service to the customers in this area, and it seemed to catch on like wildfire. We now service parts for several countries around the world. And, based on my research, I was filling a much needed niche."

"But how did you turn it into what it is today? How did you grow it into a multi-million dollar company with annual sales crossing the $100 million dollar mark with no outside help or investment?"

"Well," said Jake, "that was a labor of love. I carefully analyzed all parts of my business on a regular basis. I guess I really loved learning how I could always improve on things and make them better."

Jake folded his hands on his desk and thought about all the sleepless nights he had spent toiling away at the business. He thought about all the countless hours he had spent trying to understand and improve the company's balance sheet, minimize its taxes, and increase its profitability. He did all of this while also balancing a family life. He was a committed and devoted father, husband, and trusted member of his church community.

"Since there are a lot of people out there who admire

the successes that you've achieved, what advice would you give them in starting their own business? What are the secrets to success?"

Jake looked at the reporter sternly. He had to think about it. "Well, I guess I never really thought about what I did as anything that was too secretive. I mean, I've always believed in working hard. Sure, there are people around the world who work hard but don't seem to get ahead in life. I guess my approach has been focused hard work. I knew early on that I needed to work hard on my own business, and not work hard on making someone else rich. But, it was never really about the money to me. Sure, I wanted to be successful and live a comfortable life, but I never was intent on amassing a big fortune."

"But you've done just that. You've amassed one of the most sizeable fortunes in the state of Texas, and you're not even in the oil business."

"Yes, that's correct I suppose. Well, aside from working hard," Jake said, "I would say that to truly succeed in life you must provide something of great value to others. Not only must it be of great value, but also the value of any good or service you provide must far exceed the cost you're charging for it. As soon as the cost becomes prohibitive, the value vanishes. Sure, perceived value exists in a high price, but there isn't great value in it. To succeed you must always provide great value that's inherent, and not just perceived."

"I guess it sounds so basic, but at the heart of every large operation, exists some basic fundamental rules," said the writer. "I like the sound of that. So to succeed so far you've said that you have to work hard, work for yourself, and provide great value. Is that correct?"

"Yes. But, you don't necessarily have to be in business

only for yourself. Whether you join up with partners or whatever the case may be, you will always make more money in the long term, by running your own business. But, the difficulty with running your own business is that the beginnings are very rough. It's very difficult to get a new business off the ground, let alone save enough money to go into business for yourself in the first place. It takes a lot of discipline, and if you have high expenses and debt, the difficulty compounds itself. Because when you start a business, it's not going to be easy street. It's going to be very hard work, and you may find yourself at times wanting to quit. When you can create excuses for yourself that are fear-based such that you won't be able to cover expenses if you don't succeed, your likelihood of failing rises."

"So what would you say then to someone who had a lot of debt but still wanted to start their own business?" asked Robert.

"I think that's a difficult one. If you have a lot of debt, you have to look at why you have that debt in the first place. If you have a habit of accumulating debt, you might not have the type of mentality required to watch after your bottom line. I would say that if you still want to open your own business, first treat your life like a business. Look at everything that goes out the door monthly, and everything that comes in. Scrutinize it with detail and cut costs where necessary. Every successful business knows that it must turn a profit every month if it wants to stay solvent, and individuals should think the same way. Their lives should be looked at like balance sheets and the necessary changes and budgeting must be made in order to create long-term success."

Robert sat for a moment while digesting the information. He scribbled notes quickly, trying to keep pace with the successful business executive. He picked his head up once he finished taking his notes, and leafed back to the questions he had come prepared with to the interview. "Okay, only a few more questions, Mr. Harris."

"Please, do call me Jake."

"Right. Sorry. Jake. What other advice would you give young budding entrepreneurs who are looking to set out into the world and start their own businesses?"

"Aside from the few points I've made, I would say that the most important factors to succeeding in business are to stay humble and constantly analyze. I've seen it happen far too many times in the past where business owners get cocky and start trying to overreach, and when the markets turn for whatever reason, or the economy shifts, their businesses suffer. As a result, they face having to lay off massive portions of their workforce, or close down stores and factories. Constantly analyze and always stay humble. That's one of the critical keys to success."

"That's great advice, but if I may ask, how did you become so knowledgeable about business? Where did you get your business education? What school?"

Jake looked at the young, eager reporter. He must have been barely pushing thirty years old. Jake tried to think back to that age and just how green he was about life and business in general. He made many mistakes along the way, but he realized early on that experience in the real world far superseded anything he could learn from books.

"Well," said Jake, " I only have a high school degree. I never went to college. I don't have an MBA or some other fancy title after my name. What I have is real, hard experience. Experience that I gained from the many years of working and toiling away at my profession. I built this business over time, with hard work, perseverance, and a curiosity to always innovate and improve. Although an education may seem important to some, especially for the career-minded individuals in this world, I saw early on that the best education I would ever get was by diving in headfirst. And this is the outcome of that education."

Jake opened his arms and spread them out, indicating the sprawling complex that they were located in around them. Hundreds of thousands of square feet of office space and an enormous yard full of scrap parts being organized, prepared, cataloged, and sold around the world through the integrated systems he had pioneered.

"Wow, that's impressive. All this with no formal education," said Robert. Although the reporter knew that some of the world's wealthiest individuals barely had high school diplomas, coming face to face with one was a far different experience. It was visceral, indeed.

"In my opinion, education creates a lot of debt. Growing up, our family was poor and they taught me to save every last penny. I never squandered money when I didn't have to, which is why I still live a very frugal life. Sure, we get to enjoy a family vacation from time to time, but my focus still is, and will always be, on this business. There's something so fulfilling about it; something that goes beyond just the money and income that it produces. I'm able to see the fruits of my labor adding value to the lives of the people and customers that I come across, and that is the best part of it. That's the reason I wake up every single day."

"Yes, well, I think that you're right. But for me, I was interested in a career in journalism, and without a formal education, it's difficult to find a good position," said Robert.

"That's most likely true, but anything is possible when

you put your mind to it. Some of the most successful people in the world, whether they be writers, or business people in any field, were all self taught."

"Yes, you're right. And, had I wouldn't have been in debt up to my ears, struggling to pay it back still to this very day."

Jake looked at the young reporter with an air of concern. "Yes, debt can be extremely debilitating. It can limit you in your choices in life, and remove your freedoms. When you're facing mountains of debt, it's one of the worst possible feelings in the world. To only work in order to pay back debt, is no life at all, and I would liken it to an indentured servitude."

"Yes, it sure feels like that at times," said Robert.

"I would also say that, in business, and in life, one of the most important secrets to my success would be to always make more money than I spend, and invest it. Over time, that money compounds on itself. Over time, whatever you invest in begins to accumulate. It begins to accumulate and snowball, building an enormous amount of momentum. But, if you spend more than you make, you can never get ahead. I think that's where most people go wrong today."

"I agree. I believe that much of the world feels trapped beneath their debt."

Jake nodded at the young writer as he scratched his face. He couldn't help but think of his own youth again. It was a constant reminder of how eager he once was, just by sitting there with him.

"I just have one last question and we can wrap things up here," Robert said.

27

"Sure. Shoot. Anything."

"What are the biggest mistakes you've made in business, and if you could do it all over, what would you do differently."

Jake sat and observed the eager reporter for a moment. He thought about the answer to his question. He thought about how many souls his answers would touch and how many people his story would inspire. He thought back to all the mistakes he had made in business while trying to grow, and the different setbacks he had had. He sat for a moment thinking about it, rocking back and forth in his large, but simple chair.

"My mistakes? Well, my mistakes were plentiful. But, if I were to think about the biggest mistakes I made, they would have to be when it came to taxes. I didn't have a complete handle on my tax situation from the get go. I learned the hard way and I paid the price, but it was early on. If I were to go back and do it all over, I would have sought sound tax planning from the beginning. I would have made sure I carefully concocted a legal and tax structure that would have been most suitable for my business. Although it was a small price to pay, the lesson was an important one. That lesson taught me that small investments in sound advice early on, could make or break you. Always seek sound advice at the earliest stages. The little amount of money you'll pay will reap huge benefits later down the road."

"That's great advice," said Robert, as he got up to leave and thank Jake. "I really appreciate you taking out the time to speak to me. This was a very eye-opening experience for me. I'll be in touch via email if I have any more questions."

"Okay, no problem. Thanks for taking the time," said Jake.

"The pleasure was all mine," replied Robert as he got up, shook Jake's hand and left the sprawling complex. Jake sat in his swivel chair for a moment and tried to think back again to all the years of hard work. He realized how much he had accomplished, and thinking about it all right then and there, it felt overwhelming. There were so many sleepless nights, so many setbacks, and so many defeats that to do it all again would be hard. But, he thought about doing it all again and realized that he would do it again in a heartbeat. There was nothing more fulfilling to him than doing what he does for a living. Nothing.

*****

In today's society, most of us have come to expect instant gratification and immediate expectation of results. We want things, and we want them now, no matter what it is, whether we're talking about weight loss, more money, real-time news, high-speed Internet, or just about anything else. We want it and we want it now. In psychology, this is something referred to as the pleasure principle. Our minds are actively seeking to gain pleasure while avoiding pain. When we want something in the here and now, we're seeking instant gratification. When we want to lose weight, we want it to happen fast, not wait months or years slugging away on diets and exercise regimes. And, when we want to earn more money, we want it to happen quickly and effortlessly, without having to spend years and years planning and working towards its attainment.

Think about that for a moment. Think about your overall thought patterns on a daily basis, and think about how often your mind comes back to the anticipation of pleasurable experiences. When you've wanted something in the past, or an opportunity presented itself to you to fulfill a need quickly, how did you react? Did you jump at the chance for a 30-day weight loss program that guaranteed to shed weight fast? Did you clamor at the opportunity to buy the latest get-rich-quick scheme that you saw advertised on the television at 2 o'clock in the morning? If you have, that's okay because you're not alone. Marketers feed off our basal and instinctive nature for pleasure. They know that we want to gain pleasure and avoid pain, and they use that in their marketing material to lure us into purchasing whatever it is they're peddling.

However, this isn't a new concept. We are all the same in this respect. Every one of us is prewired to seek pleasure and avoid pain. And, we will always do more to avoid pain than we will to gain pleasure. But, different individuals go about this differently. As you may well be aware of, different personalities will have differing views on their desire for instant gratification. Some will want something immediately, without caring about the consequences. This is the most prevalent in children. Our instinctive nature as children forces us to want things without consequence. We want to eat, sleep, laugh, and cry when we want. We don't want anyone telling us we can't have or do something, because that goes against our instinctive desires for pleasure.

This instinctive notion for seeking pleasure was coined the *Pleasure Principle*, and it was introduced by the father of modern psychology, Sigmund Freud. Through his earlier works, *Project of Scientific Psychology* from 1895, and in *The Interpretation of Dreams* from 1900, he introduced us to the elements of the psyche that he deciphered through careful analysis. Freud tried to understand and interpret why we do the things that we do, and came to the realization that the basis for most human action is for the pursuit of pleasure. Most individuals are actively seeking to gain pleasure at all times. This is why the sex, drug, and alcohol industries are recession proof. It's because they are pleasure industries that satisfy our instinctive urges for pleasure.

However, as we grow and mature, the mind realizes that it can't always have what it wants. It can't always get its way every single moment of every single day. It realizes that in reality, things don't work that way. And, as children come of age, their minds develop beyond just the pleasure principle. They learn to recognize the *Reality Principle*, also coined by Freud. In reality, the mind knows that it won't be able to get its way instantly all the time, especially when it begins factoring personal economic situations into the mix. It realizes that without a certain amount of money or freedom, it can't have access to all the things it wants all of the time. The mind then begins to weigh the costs and benefits of an action in reality. It still wants the pleasure, but it realizes it must put some of the impulses and urges at bay and defer the gratification.

To better understand these concepts, and just how they affect the millionaire method, it's important to delve deep into human psychology to take a close look at the mind and its inner workings. By understanding the mind and building awareness to these processes, you can work on calling all of your mental, emotional, physical, and spiritual faculties into play in order to steer your life in the right direction. The understanding of this *Psychic Apparatus* – as coined by Freud – is critical to understanding the millionaire method. It's also because your psychology plays such an important role in your behavior and the decisions that you make in life. If you can't understand your psychology and why you do the things that you do, it's impossible to fix it.

You see, most people find psychologists when they realize that they have a substance abuse problem. They speak to psychologists to help them understand and overcome some of the deep-seeded issues that are forcing them to launch into a tirade of addictive behavior. They look for psychologists to help them deal with alcohol and drug abuse. They turn to them to help dive deep into their psyches and develop more of an understanding for their past behavior and their poor decisions. But, problems related to finances, especially when they involve excessive debt and spending, are also affected by a person's psychology. They're affected by it just as much as when a person begins to abuse any other substance, because in this case, money is being abused and not respected.

Although the abuse of money isn't causing direct physical harm to your body, it is causing an enormous amount of indirect physical harm. When you abuse money, create a lot of debt, and overspend yourself month after month, your psychology manifests stress, fear, and anxiety into your physiology. Those feelings then foster other abusive behavior, because when the money runs out, most people need something else to abuse and help them with more of the emotion-numbing behavior. As you'll come to see in the chapters of this book, this all occurs as a direct reflection of our own psychic apparatuses, which tend to take control of our lives. When that happens, we seemingly begin making poor decisions, even when we know the difference between right and wrong, and what we should be doing. It's very much similar to abusing some other substance that has a direct affect on the physiology.

But, as you may or may not already have noticed, these issues compound on themselves. Whether we're talking about the abuse of money, or anything else, they're all really just masking some of the issues hidden deep inside our minds. You see, within the first five years of life on this earth, so much of our psychology and personality takes shape. You can think of it as the core processing system for a computer. The initial setup of our minds occurs then and it hardwires a lot of our behavior for later down the road. During those first five, very influential years, so much of our personalities take shape.

Our experiences in life affect our personalities, but our

response to those experiences has a lot to do with what happened in those first five years. Those first five years are so critical that it can make two identical twins raised just a little bit differently, be opposites in every other way. Genetics does play a role in this. Your unique DNA structure has a direct affect on the way your personality takes shape. However, those experiences in life that mold us into the people that we are today can be more powerful than the underlying genetic code. Those experiences in life shape how we view the world, and how we interact with it; we adapt our minds to the world based on those experiences. The installation of our behavior and our programming happens so early on. When you can understand how the behavior works, and build awareness towards it, you'll come to the realization that you can get back into the driver's seat of your mind.

But, the mind is shrouded in a lot of secrecy. As you'll come to find, the complexity of just how the mind works has a funny way of helping support a lot of the negative behaviors that we develop. The millionaire method can't thrive in a mental environment that's unstable like this. The millionaire method must be implemented by rewiring a lot of the negative patterns of behavior you may have developed over time. But, it's quite possible to do this. It's quite possible to come to a certain understanding with yourself, by yourself, and of yourself, that will help empower you rather than limit you. That's what the millionaire method is all about. It's not about getting rich quick, or finding the hidden secrets of success. Yes, there are secrets, but they are more like basic rules and methods that you must live by in order to get ahead. You must shift your mentality from one that's expecting instant gratification, to one that's patiently awaiting deferred gratification. Eventually it will come. Eventually, you'll push through and persevere.

THE PSYCHIC APPARATUS

Sigmund Freud's contribution to modern psychology included the structural model of how the mind works within itself. The mind, separate from the brain, consists of three distinct parts, which act together in order to drive your decision-making processes. We call this structural model of the mind, the *psychic apparatus*, first discussed by Freud in a 1920 essay entitled, *Beyond the Pleasure Principle*. The psychic apparatus consists of three distinct parts which are only mental constructs of the mind, and don't actually refer to any physical parts of the brain itself. The three parts of the psychic apparatus are the id, the ego, and the superego.

These three parts of the mind play an enormous rule in influencing your behavior. They work together, but oftentimes they work against one another, making you feel internal conflict and strife. That's because, at times, they are trying to suppress one another's urges for pleasure and pain. Each one is trying to get its own way, and as an outcome, you harbor feelings of uneasiness, fear, and anxiety. This plays a tremendous role in the millionaire method, because the product of these three parts is the final behavior in how you handle your finances, and all other behavior. The product of these three parts results in your emotional and mental state of mind. The product of these three parts is critical to how you spend and save your money, and make every other decision in your life.

R.L. ADAMS

THE ID

The first part of the psychic apparatus is the id – the instinctual, native pre-programmed, and pre-conditioned behavior that's rooted in genetic survival. From the dawn of time, humankind has had the instincts, urges, and impulses to eat, sleep, and procreate. Tied to our DNA, they are intrinsic to us. These are not learned behaviors, but rather more basal and native functions. The id drives these urges and impulses based on the pleasure principle. It wants something and it wants it now. The id doesn't care for consequences, nor does it care for authority. It wants to have its way immediately, without regard for anything else.

When it comes to a discussion about finances, the id plays a very important role in your life. Anytime you have the opportunity for pleasure, your id is the driving force that's telling you to act on those urges and impulses. And, while this all occurs in the subconscious mind, it's the id that's producing those urges and impulses for you in the first place. It's the id that's telling you to lease that car you can't afford, refinance your home to take a vacation, or go out to the bar and spend your money on beer and liquor when you know you should be saving it instead. Sometimes, the id wins, but not all the time. Without the other parts of the mind, the id would always run rampant. You can see this in people who suffer general psychosis such as gamblers, alcoholics, and drug-abusers. They have less control of the other faculties of the mind that help to limit the pleasure-driven pursuits of the id.

But, money is also a construct that's highly influenced by the id. That's because money is the vehicle for virtually all of these pleasure-driven pursuits. Without money, we couldn't go off and buy drugs, alcohol, excess food, prescription drugs, or anything else that we can ingest into the body to inflict physical abuse. Money is required to do all of those things. But, money itself can also be abused. And, at the heart of all of it, whether it's money, or the things we buy with money, our inherent psychology determines our behavior. If the id is powerful enough, and it speaks loudly enough in your mind, then you may succumb to its urges. Those urges are telling you to throw all caution to the wind and follow the instinctive and basal desires for pleasure.

Anytime a pleasure-driven pursuit presents itself to you, no matter what it may be, the psychic apparatus is constantly weighing that decision in your mind. It's determining whether it can indulge in that behavior. While the id solely exists to help you satisfy your urges and impulses for pleasure, the superego, which is the second part of the psychic apparatus, helps to play more of a moral and critical role in the decisions that you make. If you've ever found yourself giving into the urges of your id, the superego is the part of your mind that makes you feel bad for allowing yourself to indulge in those decisions. For example, a person trying to save money may give into the pleasure-driven pursuits of the id when it calls them to go out and spend money on something they don't need, while the superego makes them feel bad for doing so afterwards.

You see, all these parts in the psychic apparatus are working away, constantly weighing, and analyzing things in the mind. But the id can be all-powerful. The id can be the one to drive people to commit acts they may later take for granted. It's the id that tells people it's okay to spend money, or it's okay to keep smoking cigarettes, overeating, or indulging in just about anything. When left unchecked, the id takes over the mind and it can certainly run rampant. We see this all the time in people who abuse their finances. When you know you should be saving, and instead you're spending, the id is taking control of your mind. The difficulty is that most of this happens in the subconscious mind. If you can't pay careful attention and build awareness to the processes of your mind, they will continue to control you.

THE SUPEREGO

The superego is a critical component of the mind, and without the proper development of the superego, individuals can find themselves in a spiral downwards when it comes to overindulging in detrimental behavior. But, the superego, unlike the id, forms from what's instilled in you as you're brought up as a child and into adulthood. It forms from the authority that your parents help to ingrain in you when they teach you right from wrong. It also comes from elements of society as you learn the different rules and regulations of your own locale. Moreover, it's a product of your own morality, which develops trough living and experiencing the world. It's what helps you determine good from bad, and right from wrong. For some people, their superego is virtually non-existent, which leads them to either engage in criminal behavior, or behavior that's unbecoming of a moral individual.

When the superego is virtually non-existent, we see

people constantly breaking the laws, or looking for various ways that they can get around things. If the superego doesn't properly develop, people will indulge in just about anything from substance abuse, to extramarital affairs, and the overall abuse of money and other people. We see this happen all too often, where people merely veer off course in life. They begin to take things and people for granted, and resort to ill-gotten behavior, which only helps to serve them. This is when they are doing more to gain pleasure in the short-term than they are to avoid pain in the short-term. However, once someone faces the harsh realities of their world, and they're forced to pay the consequences, reality begins to hit home, but oftentimes it's too little, too late.

The superego also develops through a person's spirituality. Through faith and a person's higher power, they come to nurture and expand their superego, allowing them to better determine just what's right and what's wrong. They use it as a baseline to help guide them through life and make the decisions that they make. It becomes part of their moral compass so-to-speak. But, the superego is a stark contrast to the desires of the id. It's exactly the opposite, and it's your mind's view of a perfect world in the sense that it acts as a conscience towards what it deems would be right in any situation. It presents your subconscious and conscious mind with the ideal behavior for any given situation, but when counterbalanced with the id, it's either vetoed or voted in. It all depends on the dominant forces of the mind for that particular time and situation.

If you've ever found yourself spending money wildly, say for example when you went on a gambling trip, or you went out to a bar, the superego is what kicks in to make you feel bad afterwards. And, the development of the superego has a lot to do with your childhood. Depending on whether you're a male or a female, and how quickly you succumbed to authoritative pressures as a child, Freud posits that the superego develops at varying rates. Therefore, if as a child, your parents had a large authority over you, and you succumbed to that authority – you weren't very rebellious – then you likely have more control over your id. Your superego is usually able to keep the id in check in this scenario. However, if you were rebellious, and you didn't have strong moral guidance as a child, then your id is likely to run more rampant.

This understanding of the psychic apparatus is critical to the millionaire method because our inherent handle on money has a lot to do with our internal psyche and how we succumb to certain urges. You can look at this on the macro level by analyzing your spending and saving habits monthly or yearly, or you can look at it on a micro level in daily decisions involving money. When you look at your decisions that affect your spending and saving on a micro level, you can better see how the superego and the id play the part there. The superego is telling you to save your money or invest it wisely, while the id is urging you to give into the impulse of leasing a shiny new car, buying some fancy jewelry, or going on a luxury vacation. When you can truly afford this type of behavior, it's okay to give into your impulses from time to time. However, when your superego clearly knows that you can't afford to do something, yet you still do it anyway, it then fills you with feelings of guilt.

In the car industry, they call this buyer's remorse. It's when you make a purchase in the heat of the moment, only later to realize that you made a big mistake. In 1972, the FTC instituted something called the *cooling off period* in order to help protect consumers who made purchases from door-to-door salesman. This 3-day period still applies to any purchases made from a company that's selling their products at a place other than their regular place of business. The product must be $25 or more, and you must inform the salesman of your right to cancel within this three-day period. However, the cooling off period doesn't apply to cars.

The main reason why they created a cooling off period in the first place, is because the FTC realized just how pushy and convincing salesman could be that came door-to-door, and how initially enticing their offers may have seemed. When you purchase an item from a salesman in this manner, or anywhere for that matter, it's very easy to allow the id to do all the thinking. That pleasure-driven pursuit that's such an aggressive part of your mind can take hold of you and not let go. The superego knows that you have responsibilities, but when the id is allowed free reign, it can trample over the superego if it hasn't developed properly. If you've ever felt major remorse for a purchase or a behavior after the fact, your superego's doing the talking.

But this remorse usually happens too late. Only after the decision is made, do the superego's feelings of remorse kick in, and not before or during. It wasn't strong enough to dissuade you from engaging in the behavior in the first place. It wasn't strong enough to keep you from spending money that you couldn't afford to spend. It wasn't strong enough from keeping the person trying to diet from driving through another fast food restaurant. It wasn't strong enough to help the alcoholic to stop drinking when he or she went to the bar again. It happens too late. If the superego doesn't properly develop, all it can really do is fill you with post-decision remorse. The goal is to have enough remorse or wherewithal prior to making the decision rather than after.

THE EGO

Although you may know of the general term *ego* as being your pride or your self, the true definition of the ego within the psychic apparatus exists within the *Reality Principle*. It acts as the referee between the id and the superego as they battle out the decision-making process in the mind. Depending on which component of the mind is stronger at the time – whether it's the id or the superego – your ultimate decision will vary. But, in essence, the ego knows that it must defer gratification for some things, because it's acting within reality. The ego knows that it can't allow you to have everything right away, but it helps to determine what it can help you have in the quickest manner possible; that's the ego's goal.

This becomes more apparent as we mature, age, and gain experiential knowledge of the world. When the ego is very young after just having been developed, it's much more eager and naïve. It thinks that it can make certain decisions without much consequence. However, as the ego shapes while we age, it realizes that, in reality things don't always work that way. It realizes that in reality things can't always come immediately. But, it attempts to create a mental state that will allow you to have what you want, as fast as you want it.

This deferred gratification championed by the ego can help you during your times of need. When the ego realizes that your financial decisions must come into reality, it will help to defer any gratification you may be seeking, by allowing you to come to a realization of the reality of your circumstances. However, for a large majority of people, the ego's decision-making process defaults to instant gratification. They want what they want, and they want it now. They are seeking pleasure, and the ego helps them find it, even when it may not be completely believable, the ego helps them find reasons why it should be believable. But, this happens to everyone. The ego will make excuses for its own decision-making process. This is why when you make a decision to purchase something, your ego looks for the reasons why you made the right decision, while the superego may make you feel guilty for it.

When you look at a person who chain smokes cigarettes, overspends, overeats, or indulges in drugs or alcohol, you may ask yourself why they do it. You may ask yourself why they make those decisions when clearly they are going to lead to more pain than pleasure. Since we do more to avoid pain than we do to gain pleasure, the decision-making process can seem skewed. An alcoholic may not understand why they overdrink, or why the person in financial ruins continues to overspend. It's because their decision-making processes are only limited to short-term causes and effects. They are doing more to avoid pain than gain pleasure in the short term, not in the long term. If they were doing more to avoid pain in the long term, then they wouldn't engage in excessive activity.

You can think back to any situations where you may have found yourself in when it came to overindulging. Whether it was food, drugs, alcohol, extra-marital affairs, and anything else, your mind was attempting to gain pleasure in the short term. This happens when the superego cannot regulate the id, which is a result of childhood rearing and life experiences. The difficulty is that your ego will make excuses for itself because it never wants to admit that what it's doing is wrong. That would go entirely against the ego itself. The inherent design of the ego is to help you make the decisions that it personally argues are the right decisions for its self. It takes into account the superego and the id to make those decisions, and it does so only based on its own personal experiences. Can you see why the psychology of the mind can have such a grave impact on spending and saving?

When the superego and the id conflict, you can be left feeling very uneasy and unsure about all your decisions. It makes the decision-making process extremely difficult. On the one hand, you have the pleasure-driven pursuits of the id urging you on. For some people, the simple thought of the instant gratification far surpasses their desire to defer their gratification for a later date. And, although they may feel conflicted at times, their sudden impulses and urges will overcome the superego's call for more calm, cool, and collected minds. However, afterwards, the superego institutes extreme feelings of guilt, leaving you with a very uneasy feeling about the decisions you're making.

As you can now see, the psychic apparatus's infighting in your mind can be exacerbating, to say the least. It's no wonder why we have such conflicting feelings when it comes to our pursuit of pleasure. But, in order to master the millionaire method, you must start at the psychic apparatus level since it's really the driver in the car called your life. The mind, with its psychic apparatus, is steering and controlling your life, the decisions that you make, and the behavior that you embark upon. Since those resultant behaviors control the outcome of our lives, the psychic apparatus is at the heart of all that we do, and all that we are. The ego is constantly weighing decisions by attempting to balance all three components of the psychic apparatus.

In order to master your financial life and start on the road to wealth building, you must first master your psychic apparatus. The difficulty is however, that most of this self-talk which occurs in your mind, is purely subconscious. The id is a purely subconscious construct, and both the ego and superego live in both the conscious and subconscious realms of your mind. So in order to be able to recognize the self-talk that's going on, and to take control of it, you must learn to build awareness. You build awareness by paying attention to your emotions, because your emotions are the gateway to your thoughts. Learning to recognize and understand those emotions is the key to unraveling your psychic apparatus.

When you can pay acute attention to your emotions, you know what's going on in your mind, and you can work to retrace those thoughts that led to those emotions. Why did you start feeling that way? What sparked that initial feeling inside of you? If you started to feel fearful, what set you on that path of thought? Think about it carefully. If you can clue into those emotions, and you can look at them with an honest, and open frame of mind, you can begin to unravel the true inner workings of your mind. If you can't look at it with an honest, and open awareness, then doing so will become significantly more difficult.

EXERCISING THE PSYCHIC APPARTUS

Try this for a moment; try to pay acute awareness to your emotions. Once you finish reading this chapter, sit still for several minutes. Take as much time as you can take, and turn off all the distractions. Shut everything else off, from your phone, to the Internet, the television, and anything else. You have to do this when you have alone time. If you're interrupted, it won't help you. It won't help because the mind will just get confused with more things to do. You have to clear your mind, and sit still. If you've never sat still before, you may find this difficult. That's because when you're sitting still, you're aware, and your ego doesn't want you to be aware. It wants to make decisions on its own without the interference of the conscious mind.

After you've sat still for a while, your mind will begin churning and thinking. The subconscious will begin rattling away at all the things going on in your life. It will start weighing experiences and the things around you, along with your relationships, and finances. Pay careful

47

attention to your emotions at this time. Grab a pen and paper to have it near by, and write down any of the emotions that you feel. Write out just how you're feeling and what made you feel that way. Did you feel anxious? What made you feel those feelings? Are you fearful of something? Maybe not having enough money to pay your bills at the end of the month? Maybe not having enough money to retire? What thoughts led you to that fear? Try to retrace them.

This is an excellent exercise for the mind. It's an excellent way for you to peer into the inner workings of your psychic apparatus. Try to trace back and weigh out that thought-pattern. See if you can recognize the voices in your head. Can you recognize what the pleasure-seeking id is telling you to do? Can you recognize what the authority-seeking superego is telling you to do? These components, or forces, are the voices in your head. The reality principle in the ego balances these forces. What did the ego say to you? How did the ego tell you that you could solve your issues in your life while still getting what you wanted? What compromises is it presenting you with as options? This inner wrangling can be so interesting. It can be so interesting to help shed awareness, and see the truth of what your mind is actually thinking. When you look at it from this perspective, and realize that the worst situation isn't actually that bad, you can work towards resolving it.

Even if you're facing a scary situation, you must realize that many people in the past have faced the same or similar situation, and have overcome it. Many people in the future will also face that same or similar situation. Fear-based thoughts won't serve you, and in fact, it will just foster more physiological problems. The stress, fear, and anxiety wreak havoc on your body. Try to look at your situation from a bird's-eye view. Think back to other times in your life when you were in a bad situation, but you were able to pull yourself out of it. The strong emotions that take hold of your body are only the result of the ego blinding you to the truth. When you can look at the truth, and see it for what it is, then take steps towards fixing it, you'll feel remarkably better. However, if you continue to feel the emotions, yet don't do anything about it, then it will only get worse.

This exercise doesn't just apply to helping your emotions when it comes to finances; it applies to fixing anything else in your life. Whatever it is that's bothering you, your mind is well aware of it. It's front and center stage in the theater of your mind, and it's weighing all of its options in your subconscious. But, when you choose not to act, or do anything about it, the mind becomes frustrated. The superego is screaming for you to do something, yet so is the id, and in between, you have your ego trying to grapple amongst them all. Make the decision to understand your emotions, and retrace your thoughts, and you will feel remarkably better. You'll realize that it's not as bad as it seems because knowledge is power. Once you have the knowledge, you have the power to fix your situation. By keeping yourself in the dark, you're only helping to foster more shrouding by the ego, which then helps to spin you further into a tailspin.

The exercise isn't difficult, and you should do it on a daily basis, or multiple times a day if necessary. As soon as you start feeling emotions that begin to overpower you, stop what you're doing, and do the exercise. If you're alone this is much easier to do. If you're not, try to jot down quickly what you were feeling for later analysis. Then, when you're alone, try to retrace those emotions and thoughts. It's best to do it when it happens, but if you can't, then save it for a later time. But, makes sure you do it. This is an important part of understanding your psyche, because when you can understand the inner wrangling and shed light on it, you can work to fix the problem. Don't try to understand it, and you'll continue to feel uneasy about things.

Remember, fear and anxiety are the body's warning signals. It's trying to warn you that something is wrong, so you have to go digging. Don't just sit there and allow yourself to feel uneasy. Try to understand what's truly bothering you. Try to unearth those thoughts and trace them back to their origins. This can be difficult, but it's not impossible. Pay very close acute attention to your emotions and your thoughts in this exercise, and retrace them. Retrace them to see what's really on your mind. What is it that's really bothering you? Is it truly that bad? What steps can you take to fix it? Usually, these issues are at the heart of our emotion-numbing activities. When you can't resolve the internal conflicts in your mind, you default to more emotion-numbing activities. Be aware, and work to resolve your internal conflicts. Without doing so, you can't truly implement the millionaire method.

2

THE PSYCHOLOGY OF DEBT

"A man in debt is so far a slave." – Ralph Waldo Emerson

Jonathan Snow woke up to the incessant sound of his alarm clock. It was 6:30am. He thought about smashing the contraption on the floor, but didn't want to pay for a new one again. It was early, far too early to be getting up. However, Jonathan had no choice because he was mired in debt, and weighed down by financial obligations that had him drowning in a pool of interest rates, and monthly payments. He had managed to max out all of his credit cards, and was facing a financially cataclysmic situation. He wasn't sure how he was going to afford to pay his bills, which were due in the matter of only a few short days.

He walked into the bathroom and washed his face. His head was pounding. He had spent the night with friends, drinking and playing poker. It was a weekly ritual. But, Jonathan's weekly rituals were plentiful, and they had started to catch up with him. He was leading a life filled with pleasure-driven pursuits that occupied nearly all of his free time. There was no time dedicated to planning or strategizing his future, never in the past, and never in the foreseeable future. Those activities took the backburner in his mind. Although he knew he had to do something about pulling his life together, he never could tear himself away from the other activities he preferred over that. He would much rather be spending time with friends, somewhere out and about, than sitting home and grinding away at his future.

All Jonathan Snow wanted to do was have fun. He didn't want to look at his situation, and just how bad it was. He didn't want to come to the realization of just how bad things had gotten. He wasn't sure how it had happened, but it did. And, as he looked into the mirror, he realized the reality of his situation that morning. He was drowning, and he was barely able to keep his head above water. He was drowning in a sea of debt, and he couldn't swim. His creditors were strangling him, and they were trying to wring him for every last red cent he had. He wasn't sure how much longer he could take the feeling. He wasn't sure just how much longer he would last.

He washed his face, and the sting from the cold, wet water evaded his mind, sending shooting pains throughout his brain. All he could hear was the thumping inside his head, viciously vibrating, and pulsating away. He could feel the incessant echo of that thump ratcheting every cell in his body as it pounded through his skull. He could barely see straight. He tried to look into the mirror, but with vision blurred, he struggled to adjust. It was one of the worst hangovers he had experienced in a long time.

Only two hours of sleep, how am I going to make it through this day?

He struggled with that thought as he brushed his teeth. The pounding headache led to ringing in his ears. Things were only going to get worse.

I need to lie back down, but I can't. Why, oh why do I have to subject myself to this life-sucking job?

The thoughts that ran through his mind that morning were no different from the thoughts that ran through his mind most mornings. He was sick and tired of being sick and tired, but he was trapped. He was a rat in the race of life, and he was losing. Each month he would get further and further behind, drowning deeper in debt, and losing any sense of himself. To cope, he turned to distractions that only helped to drive him further into the hole he was digging for himself.

All of those thoughts were running through Jonathan's mind as he brushed his teeth and tried to get his bearings. All of those thoughts evaded his mind and took over. He couldn't think straight, he couldn't see straight, and he certainly wasn't sure how we was going to work in that manner. But, he had no choice. He knew he had to go in and put up with yet another life-sucking day at a job he didn't want to have anymore. He knew he had to go in and deal with it; he was a product of his own choices. His bad choices led him to where he was, and nothing else.

After getting ready, Jonathan headed into his kitchen to grab a quick meal before he left. He opened the fridge to realize it was empty. He spent most of his meals eating out and would always forget to stock the fridge for meals at home. His life of eating out only led to accumulating more debt, and he was barely hanging on. He surveyed the shelves of the fridge and cursed himself for not being more careful. He scanned through the bad leftovers he had failed to discard and shook his head.

Jonathan closed the refrigerator and leafed through the stack of mail he had been avoiding, which had accumulated on the kitchen table. Bills and offers for credits. He opened up the offers for credit to see if he could score another credit card. He decided he would fill it out after work, in an attempt to keep up with his costly lifestyle, because otherwise, he really had no choice. He had no choice but to rack up more debt. He had no choice but to pile on the revolving payments; it was the only way to survive. It was the only way he could hang on to any semblance of normalcy in the messed up thing he called his life.

Where am I going to get the money to pay for rent this month?

Jonathan's poker playing and drinking last night wasn't only a bad decision because of the hangover the next day, but it also was financially costly. After six hours of drinking and playing cards, he was down seven hundred dollars. He had lost a large part of his rent payment. He knew he should have stopped halfway through, but in an attempt to win his money back, he lost it all. He had promised himself he would only lose up to two hundred dollars, but once again, he had broken his own promises to himself.

Jon took a swig from a carton of milk he had removed from the fridge, only to spit it out into the sink. He looked at the carton – expired three days ago. He cursed the milk and his life as he walked outside to his car, in the apartment's outdoor covered parking area. He got in, turned the ignition and the car wouldn't start.

Piece of crap car, please, please don't do this to me this morning!

After five minutes of trying to start his car, the engine finally turned over. He had been promising himself he would take it in for repairs, but somehow he just never seemed to find the time. Jonathan had neglected his car, just as he had neglected everything else in his life. He realized the severity of his decisions as everything compounded on one another that morning. He realized just how much he had neglected all the things that mattered.

On the long commute into work, Jonathan thought about his life, and the situation he was in. He thought about all the other things that he had hoped he would be doing at his age. He thought about all the missed opportunities and rejections of his past, and thought about what his life would have been like if he hadn't given up. You see, Jonathan gave up on many things in his life. He gave up on business, he gave up on marriage, he gave up on friends, and he gave up on family. His string of giving up was a spiraling spin in the wrong direction, and he was heading for complete self-destruction.

However, each time he told himself he was going to make a change, somehow he slipped back into the negative patterns. Somehow, he allowed his bad behaviors to get the best of him. He didn't even trust himself enough to make those promises anymore. He knew he would just break them. He knew that no matter what he said, he always acted differently. As soon as the opportunity afforded itself, he would rush back into an indulgent lifestyle. In the past, he had managed to dig himself out of debt. But, as soon as he had done so, he found a way to climb right back into it. It was a vicious and never-ending cycle.

He kept thinking about the severity of his situation as he walked into the office fifteen minutes late. Normally, fifteen minutes late wasn't a big deal. Employees could make it up at the end of the day. But, Jonathan had a habit of being late. Not only did he have a habit of being late, but his sales were also weak, which further compounded his situation at the office. He was the lowest-producing salesperson in the three-hundred-employee call center where he worked.

He looked up at the white fluorescent light bulbs as he quickly rounded the corner towards his very small cubicle, and he felt the life sucked right out of him again. The life-sucking energy from the fluorescent light bulbs, coupled with the still raging hangover, made Jonathan curse his life under his breath again. He cursed all that it was, and all that he had become. He felt miserable as he walked the long and unenergetic hallways to his cubicle. He felt like the most infinitesimal being on the planet. It was at that point that he felt his breaking point nearing. He knew he couldn't hang on much longer, he just didn't know how much longer he could muster living that life.

He looked around as he slumbered down the long cubicle-lined hallway to his own spot somewhere in the massive maze of workspaces. He breathed a sigh of relief. Ears ringing, head pounding, Jonathan logged onto his computer and phone system to review the monthly sales charts, and realized just how below average his performance had been. There was no way he would be able to meet his monthly quota at that rate. And, without meeting the monthly quota, he risked losing his job, and further risked being unable to pay his debt and support his lifestyle.

Jonathan sighed as he stared at the glaring white screen. The words didn't make sense. His vision blurred for a moment, and he couldn't see straight. Although he was used to the humming chatter of the call center, all of a sudden the voices sounded so loud. They rang in his head. Pounding. Ringing. Shooting pains. The major affects of a night spent slacking off were starting to hit home, and they were starting to hit home hard. He thought back to how much fun he had just the night before, and how he knew he would be cursing life the next morning. Yet still, he continued drinking and playing cards; he continued driving himself deeper and deeper into the hole he had dug.

He tried to concentrate. He placed his headset on his head and braced himself for the inbound phone calls. He didn't even have the energy to see straight let alone make sales. How was he going to do it? How was he going to muster up the energy to move forward? How was he ever going to be able to quit his life-sucking job and pay off his mountain of debt? Why couldn't he just be rich? Why oh why?

*****

Success theories are plentiful. There are boundless books, television shows, radio stations, courses, programs, websites, and resources dedicated to success. Most of them tout purchasing some program, or signing up to some system, in order to create a life of abundance and become financially free. But, we all know it's not as easy as that; we all know that it takes much more than some course to become financially free – it takes a complete life overhaul.

The difficulty today is that many people are merely trying to scratch the surface of income generation. They're trying to place a Band-Aid in a place where major surgery is required, because they're not addressing the underlying causes of how they got to where they are in the first place. They're not addressing the root causes of the largest limiting factor to succeeding in today's world: debt.

To most people, the word debt is a bad word. It's a word that's so frowned upon by so many people who are straddled and imprisoned by it, that merely uttering the word puts them on edge. And, rightfully so, because the world is mired in debt. Most of the global population is swimming in a sea of never-ending bills, revolving payments, and ballooning interest rates. To keep up with their lifestyles, people often need to incur more debt just to pay off their present debt, a vicious cycle that leads nowhere but into a deep dark hole with seemingly no end in sight.

But, what is it that causes us to create mounting debt in the first place? What is it about life that forces us onto the Hedonic treadmill in a ceaseless cycle of debt payments that seem to always catch up to and outpace income? How is that even though people seem to get ahead at times, they never seem to stay ahead? If any of these questions sound familiar to you, you're not alone. You're not alone because much of the world faces this situation. Most of the people wake up to another day where they have to struggle in the face of insurmountable debt. They struggle with the demands of living a lifestyle that they've become so accustomed to. They struggle with all of this, and as their debt mounts, they begin to realize the severity of their situations. They begin to realize just how bad things have gotten, and how much worse things could get.

Still, others out there refuse to be honest with themselves about their situations. They refuse to take a good hard look at their financial pictures, and just how much debt they face. They choose not to look at it because, if they do, they would experience an enormous amount of pain. And, we do a lot more to avoid pain than we do to gain pleasure, but it's our psychic apparatus that keeps us in that debt spiral. Our ego helps to shroud the truth of our real financial picture from us. For most people, to face the real truth means admitting that much of what they've believe and worked towards was all for naught, as they come to grips with the reality of their situations. It would mean an enormous amount of pain.

However, we do need to be realistic about our situations. We need to take a good hard look and understand how the psychology of debt – or how you look at spending and saving in the first place – plays such a major role in your potential success in life. Eliminating debt is one of the most important factors in the millionaire method, because no matter what your income is, your debt can always catch up to and outpace it. Without getting a handle on why you accumulate that debt in the first place, you won't have the tools to get ahead in life. But, by understanding the reasons why you make the decisions that you do when it comes to spending and debt, you can work towards understanding and correcting the problems before they continue to balloon further out of control.

We've all seen the reports featuring the glaring renditions of celebrities, and famed businesspersons alike, who've lost it all. From flying high and riding life's wave where nothing could go wrong, to the bottom of the heap, we witness their falls from grace. Nothing could have stopped them until they were sucked into some addictive behavior, or overspent beyond their means, and were trapped when the rug was pulled from beneath them. For whatever reason, a combination of negative and addictive behaviors brought them back down to earth. It happens all the time, all around the world, and no matter who you are or how much money you make, debt can always be your downfall.

No matter what day and age we're living in – whether we're just emerging from a financial crisis, or riding an economic high – debt seems to be the biggest plague in putting a wrench in success. Whether we're talking about the success of a country, a business, or a person, it's all the same. Debt plagues those places, businesses, and persons, and holds them back from attaining true financial freedom. However, when it comes to a business, they tend to understand their income and expenses. With good accounting, they can see where the money is going to and where the money is coming from. This is the basis of profits and losses in a nutshell. In addition, businesses are more accountable to their income and losses when there are shareholders involved. However, individuals are less likely to do so. Individuals are less likely to operate their lives like a business. Most individuals don't know how much money they spend each month. They may have a rough estimate, but usually, they don't have the specifics. They choose to ignore the specifics.

But, no matter what we're talking about – places, businesses, or persons – a clear understanding of why you make the decisions that you make when it comes to money and spending, is critical for achieving success. You have to understand why you're deciding to spend money on something today, which you'll need to work for years to pay off in the future. You have to understand those decisions, especially when the item you're purchasing is beyond your means and becomes a depreciating asset. Real estate aside, we all know about the depreciating assets. Whether it's a luxury car, a boat, or some other big-ticket item, they only serve to help our egos. They serve to help us show off that we can afford something today that we have to pay for in the future.

What's worse is, spending money frivolously on things that aren't even assets. I'm talking about the exotic vacations, the nights out on the town, and any and all other addictive behavior fueled by money. This not only costs money in the short term, but it hurts in the long term. It hurts because this is money that can be spent to help pay off debts, and invest in the future. But, when the ego runs rampant, it's difficult to see the forest through the trees. It's hard to see the bigger picture, when all you want to do is just have a good time. But the good times catch up with you eventually. Eventually, the good times begin to be outpaced by the bad as life catches up and reality hits home.

When we allow debt to run our lives, it doesn't matter how much income we can generate. It doesn't matter because the debt can merely cancel out the income. You can continue to make more money, but if your spending doesn't cease, there will never be an end in sight. But, there's so much involved with spending and debt that stems from our psychology; there's so much personal internal wrangling that happens when we make those decisions, that without understanding why we do the things we do, we can never truly tackle our debt. If we do tackle it temporarily, it will only be racked back up again at a later date because the true emotions and feelings weren't dealt with in the first place that led to the spending and debt. By dealing with the psychological aspects of debt, you can help to eliminate it once and for all.

UNDERSTANDING YOUR DEBT

Not many people like to talk about their debt, and rightfully so. Sometimes, it's easier not to know just how much debt you have, or how much of your monthly net income goes towards paying off that debt. There's a certain sweet and savory sense involved with playing ignorant. However, that will only get you so far. And, more importantly, the more you don't understand your own debt situation, the more likely your debt will continue to balloon out of your control as time goes on.

It's easy to allow debt to get out of control. It's easy to allow it to take over your life, but it doesn't have to be that way. However, if you continue to ignore your debt situation, then it will only get worse. It won't get better if you don't work to understand it and its root causes. The more you allow time to drag by, the more dire the situation is going to get. That's because problems become more difficult to deal with as time passes by. We get used to simply ignoring them, and as they sit on some shelf, they begin to grow more, and more, until we have no choice but to look at them. But, at that point, it's usually too little too late.

However, if you're serious about succeeding financially, the first thing you need to do is create a lay of the land so to speak. You have to outline your present debt and income situation. How much debt do you really have? What are your total monthly expenses? How much are your interest rates for each of your revolving lines of credit? You have to take a close and detailed look at these. You can't choose to ignore them any further if you're serious about succeeding with the millionaire method. If you're serious about achieving your financial goals, you have to first take an honest look at your present financial situation, and go from there. Without assessing your current situation, you can't arguably gauge where you are, or how far you have to go to reach your goals.

Your debt and your exact monthly expenses are not things that you can guestimate. If you don't have the exact numbers, overestimate, but you have to start somewhere. You have to start by outlining your present situation, no matter how bad it may be. You have to look at your financial picture from a very honest perspective, and spell it out for yourself. Lay it all out in front of you. How bad is it? If it's really that bad, then you really do need to do this. You need to shock yourself into realizing just how bad you've allowed things to get, because if you don't do this then you'll continue along on the same path, and things will only get worse.

Once you have the picture there in front of you, understand that there are many ways that you can actually reduce your monthly debt – clever tactics used by debt consolidation firms to help you tackle your monthly payments. However, instead of placing the burden on another company to help you, you must do this on your own. There's nothing wrong with being honest and forthright with your own self, even if the situation is very bad. No matter who you are and how much debt you have, there's always someone else who's been in a similar situation or worse than you. The important thing to remember is that, if you plan to extricate yourself from that situation, you have to be completely honest with yourself.

The hardest part about climbing out of a mountain of debt is being honest with yourself. If everyone was able to take a very candid look at their own situation, they might modify their behavior enough to not accumulate additional debt. However, the ego does a lot to shroud and hide you from the truth because in its eye, it's trying to protect you from experiencing pain. Remember, you do more to avoid pain than you do to gain pleasure. But, you have to also be aware that by avoiding that pain in the short term, you're going to be creating more pain in the long term. You have to look to the long-term pain as opposed to the short-term pain, if you're going to get ahead. But, the ego has a tendency to only act within the here and now. It doesn't want you to weigh the long-term causal effects. It only wants you to see the short-term causal effects.

OUTLINING YOUR INCOME, DEBT, AND EXPENSES

The first step in assessing your financial situation, then, is to be honest and straightforward with yourself. Do this by outlining your income, debt, and expenses on a single piece of paper. Place the paper horizontally, and draw two-lines, vertically separating the page into three areas. Once you have your separations, write down all of your monthly income, debt, and expenses. For your income, be sure to use your disposable income (the income that you can spend after taxes). If you aren't self-employed, this is usually simple to calculate. You just take your total monthly income, which already includes your monthly deductions, along with any other sources of income you may have, and place the total figure in the first box.

The second box should include all of your revolving debt (i.e. credit card debt, lines of credit, etc.), which you should list in order from highest interest rate, to lowest interest rate, along with your fixed debt in the third box. Separating your revolving debt from your fixed debt is important, since your revolving debt will be the priority at first. The revolving debt is the biggest burden for most people. For example, you may have some car loans, rent, and other payments, but these will go into the third column as fixed debt and expenses. The second column should only include debt that is revolving and can change from month to month.

Write down, in order from top to bottom, the highest interest rate revolving debt you have, working your way down to the lowest interest rate revolving debt you have. Be sure to also include the total outstanding balance and the monthly payments for each of these debts on your worksheet. And, be honest with yourself. Don't skip any debts, including any personal loans you've taken from friends or family. Personal loans from friends and family should always be paid back first. If someone close to you such as a friend or a loved one trusted you enough to lend you money, don't betray that trust by not paying him or her back in a timely manner. That should be a top priority for you.

Once you've detailed all of your revolving debt, list off all of your fixed debt and monthly expenses in that third box. This would include all your monthly and fixed rate expenses that you have, such as health insurance, car insurance, car payments, groceries, meals and entertainment, travel, and so on. To do this, you need to gather up six months of your past bank statements and go through each one with a fine toothcomb. Average out your expenses in each of the categories. Are you spending too much on bank fees and overdrafts? That should be the first indication that you're skating on thin ice. If you're going into a bank overdraft, or you're borrowing money from payday advance loans, then you're in very dangerous territory of succumbing to financial ruin.

On your piece of paper now, you should have your total income, revolving debt, and your fixed debt plus monthly expenses. Take a careful look at it now. If you haven't done this exercise, then you need to stop reading and do it now. It's critical that you take mental control of your financial situation, because the more you choose to ignore it, the worse it will get. When you look at your financial picture, your ego can't hide from itself. But it will do whatever it can to make you ignore it, because it knows that the more you ignore it, the more you will succumb to the pleasurable pursuits of the id. And, since you will do more to avoid pain than you will to gain pleasure, if you truly know what your financial picture is then you can no longer hide from it. You're going to want to do more to avoid the pain of how dire it may have gotten by starting to fix it.

Once you can see the reality of your financial picture in front of you, it should instill more pain than pleasure. That's because once you can see the gravity of your present situation, you should realize that you have a lot of work to do. This will force you to be more honest with yourself, and not slip back into the pleasure-driven pursuits of the id when it beckons you to spend more money on unnecessary and extraneous purchases. You should not only paint your financial picture right now, you should make a habit of doing this each month for the next six months. It takes six months of consistently doing something to form a habit, and if you analyze your financial picture each month for the next six months, or even twelve months, and set some clear financial goals for yourself, you'll no longer be able to hide from the truth. The truth will be right in front of you, and it should force you to push through your present-day limitations. And, even though it may involve some short-term pain to paint the picture right now, it will lead to long-term gain as you work to correct the problems down the road.

So, take a good look at it now and keep this sheet of paper handy, because it's going to play a critical role in setting your financial goals. All too often, people simply tend to ignore their financial picture, but when you have it staring straight at you, it's glaringly impossible to ignore. It's right there in front of your eyes. And, now that it's right in front of you, add up all of your debt and expenses on a monthly basis. How much are you spending just to service your debt? Mortgage or rent aside, how many revolving debt payments do you have? How much are you paying per month in interest payments and how much of your principle balance are you paying off each month? If you don't know the answers to these questions, it's time to start digging and analyzing.

Although at first glance they may seem small, these little charges add up across the board. If you're getting charged money each time you take an advance on your credit card, or each time you have an overdraft fee, these can amount to hundreds of dollars per month. That's money you can be using to help pay down your debt, rather than put yourself in a worse-off situation. Look at the numbers carefully. Add every category up and look at the average over the past six months. Be completely open and honest with yourself, and share the figures with a spouse or a loved one. Make sure that you take some responsibility and are held accountable for your spending habits going forward. If you know that you can't only rely on yourself, then elect the help of someone close to you. If you're afraid of others judging you for your debt, don't be, because everyone has problems. It's okay to not be perfect. There's nothing out there that says you have to be perfect all the time, it's just a fabrication of the ego. Moreover, it's much more honorable to come clean about your financial picture, and then make strides to fix it, than it is to keep hiding from it.

GETTING OUT OF DEBT

The first and most important rule there is to getting out of debt is to not take on any additional debt. If you're having a hard time supporting your existing debt, then there's a major problem. If you're making the bare minimum just to pay off your minimum monthly payments, then your likelihood of extricating yourself from your mountain of debt is going to be challenging. But, if you're honest enough with yourself to see the financial picture that you've created, then you can take steps in correcting the problems rather than further exacerbating them.

For some people, it's hard not to create additional debt, especially when their lifestyles require a certain amount of spending or debt creation. This only leads to debt acceleration – the quickening of debt accumulation over time – and to more difficulty in paying off that debt. This is where the financial picture that you painted in the previous step will come into play. The first thing you need to do is eliminate any extraneous expenses that you can afford to cut out of your life. If you say you can't afford to cut down your meals & entertainment budget, then you're lying to yourself. Be honest, and make the necessary changes, because without doing so, you will continue to wallow away in debt.

The financial picture that you created with your income, debt, and expenses, should allow you to get a good overview of where the money is going every month. Some people simply lose track of their spending because they don't pay close enough attention. This type of behavior also results in more bank fees and overdrafts when the bank declines or returns charges. Don't put yourself into this situation. Cut down your monthly expenses so that you're spending less each month than you make. If you consistently spend more each month than you make, you won't be able to climb out of debt. Yes, your life is going to be a little bit less exciting without the extraneous spending, but the more you plan now, the better your days will be to come. The less you plan now, the worse your days will be to come.

To most people, this is the hardest part about getting out of debt. Spending less money than they are normally accustomed to is what takes the most effort in getting used to. Simply put, people don't want to have to delay gratification. They don't want to have to put off until tomorrow, what they can have, or do today. The pleasure-driven pursuits of the id are constantly revving the engine of your mind. It's telling you to go out, spend that money, and worry about the consequences later. Well, later is right now. If you don't plan and do something about it, the problem will only get worse. If you don't plan then your future won't be bright; it will be dim and full of a lot more toil and unrelenting struggle.

Take a look at the financial picture and tally up all the totals. What's your total outstanding debt due? How much money do you owe people out there? What's your net worth? Do you have any assets worth speaking of? It's a difficult pill to swallow for some, but the net worth number is an important number to track. It's important because, as the months and years go by, you can use it as a barometer to gauge where you are in life. Don't beat yourself up over it; just take a good honest look at your situation, and work to fix it. Work to thrive, and not just survive. If you're just surviving, then life is more than likely weighing heavily on you. I know how difficult things can get sometimes, but there's more out there. You're meant to achieve so much more. Don't allow the pressures of life to get you down.

The next step in getting out of debt after you've allocated areas where you can save money each month, is to pay off your highest rate revolving debt first. With the additional money that you save by eliminated some of your expenses, you can pay off some of the high interest rate debt that's dragging you down. Since your highest rate monthly payment is costing you the most money in the long term, to tackle your hefty debt load, pay off the highest rate cards or loans first, then work your way down. On the list you created, where you listed off your monthly debt in order of highest to lowest interest rate, begin at the top.

If you can afford to double your monthly minimum payments for your highest interest rate monthly debt, you will quicken the pace to paying off that debt and climbing out of the hole. Once you've paid off the highest interest rate revolving debt, move onto the next one, and then keep going down the list. Each month ensure that you track your financial picture so that you can get a lay of the land. Are you improving from month to month? How about week to week? The more obsessive you are over your spending, debt, and income, the more likely you'll be able to quickly progress. And, once you get in the habit of eliminating expenses and debt, it will become like second nature to you. You won't have to think about it in the

R.L. ADAMS

future; you'll just do it. Furthermore, as you pay off each debt, the successes of your progress will compound on one another, further motivating you to push forward. At first, it will be hard, but as the months go by, your progress will quicken. Slow and steady will win the race here. There's no magical bullet or formula.

The other thing that I would suggest is, if you do have many high interest rate credit cards, and you're able to tap your home mortgage to pay off the high interest rate cards, make sure you cut up those credit cards. The biggest problem that people face when they use home equity to pay off revolving high interest debt is that, pretty soon they slip right back into debt. Those shiny credit cards that once seemed so dreadful, now become instantly more attractive. The pleasure-driven id will beckon you to jump back into spending. If you know you can't trust yourself, don't go down this road. But, cancelling those cards is also not a good thing for your credit report. It's better to have seasoned accounts with less than 30% of the balance outstanding on your credit report to help bolster your score. By closing accounts that are paid off, you'll only lower your credit score. Yes, I know, this is a double-edged sword, and not spending money takes discipline, but you have to make it a priority. Cut up the cards if you don't trust yourself, but keep the accounts open, saving one card for emergency spending.

Keep in mind that getting out of debt is not easy. There are many people out there that tout easy ways out of debt, but without risking major damage to your credit score, there really is no easy way out. You have to make sure that you educate yourself when it comes to your credit and your overall debt. From home mortgages, to debt refinancing, to interest rates, and everything else, the more you know, the better you'll be at making informed decisions when it comes to managing your finances. Also, remember that you can renegotiate interest rates on revolving debt. As long as you're not missing monthly payments, or paying late, you can usually renegotiate or ask for a lower interest rate, especially if your financial situation has changed recently.

Don't listen to your id when it comes to making decisions that will poorly affect your financial health. Make sure that your decisions are informed, sound decisions, to help you move up the financial ladder of success. As you may have already come to find out, emerging from debt is incredibly hard. Yes, we all want to find that magic bullet, or secret recipe to accomplishing something, but aside from winning the lottery, or receiving an unexpected windfall of cash through an inheritance or court ruling, earning money and getting out of debt takes hard work. It takes consistent effort and discipline to emerge from a mountain of debt. But, if you can instill enough discipline in yourself to accomplish this, it will empower you like never before.

SETTING FINANCIAL GOALS

What are your financial goals? For each person, his or her goals are a little bit different. Each person has their own specific financial vision for themselves. Whatever your financial goals may be you have to write them down. Why write them down? Well, something visceral happens when you actually write down your goals. This doesn't just apply to setting financial goals, it applies to setting any goals you may have in life. When you write them down, and you can see them in front of you, they become that much more real. They suddenly take on a different form as they glare right back at you. It can either help force you to see how far you are behind, or help motivate you on a daily basis.

Now that you've painted your financial picture for yourself, it's time to decide where you want to be one month, one year, two years, five years, ten years, and on from now. Decide for yourself just how much money you plan on making, just how much debt you want to have, and what your total intended net worth will be. First, do your most long-term goal. Set a 10-year goal for yourself. If you want to have a million dollars in net worth, make a

10-year, or longer-term goal for yourself. If you're looking at being more aggressive, try 5 years. Afterwards, break that goal down into stages, and shorter-term milestones. If you want one million dollars in net worth ten years from now, how much do you plan to have five years from now? How about one year from now?

When you break apart your goals into milestones, they become much more manageable. One million dollars in net worth over ten years means that you must increase your net worth by one hundred thousand dollars per year. What will you do to earn that money? What plans do you have to eliminate those expenses? How will you produce that added income? Will it be by starting a new business? How about by investing in stocks, bonds, commodities, or anything else? Whatever it is, create a plan. With a plan, you're much more likely to allow your mind to begin searching for ways it can achieve your goals. Without a plan, they are just abstract numbers. When you write out a plan, it becomes more real. The ideas begin to take real shape in your mind.

Find a Strong Enough Reason Why

In order to accomplish your financial goals, it takes more than just writing out a game plan. It takes more than just setting milestones and coming up with a plan of action to achieve your goals. In order to achieve your financial goals, you have to come up with strong enough reasons why you want to achieve them. What is it about your goals that make you want to achieve them? Is it just because you want to have more money? If that's the case, it won't be strong enough to overcome the pleasure-driven pursuits of the id. No, you have to have a very powerful meaning as to why you **must** achieve your goals.

In order to make your goals a must, you have to have a strong enough reason why you want to achieve them. Is it because you want to have the freedom to go where you want, and spend the time you want with your children, or spouse? Maybe it's because you want to help support your family who has stuck by your side for all these years. Whatever it is, it has to be strong enough to push you through your present-day limitations. It has to be strong enough to help you overcome your obstacles, even in the face of so much temptation. It has to be strong enough to help you get through any adversity that you may be faced with in life.

When you have a strong enough reason why you must achieve your financial goals, the obstacles melt away; they become unimportant and easily surmountable. That's because you know why you're doing what you're doing. It's not for some obscure purpose. You have a strong reason for doing it. When your reason is strong enough, you can overcome anything. When your reason is strong enough, no matter what happens to you, or what setbacks and failures you face, you'll power through it. Come up with a strong enough reason why, and write them out. Put it somewhere you can see it, and read it everyday when you wake up and before you go to bed. Emblazon those reasons into your mind's eye so that you see them every time you're tempted to give up or lose sight of your financial goals.

The more passion you put behind your reasons, the more likely you'll be to push harder and harder towards your goals. Take the time and write out a full page in passionate prose, why you want to achieve your goals. Go into specific details. Type it out and hang it on your mirror in your bathroom, or on your refrigerator in your kitchen. Put it somewhere you can see it every single day, and read it aloud with passion. Say it like you mean it, and repeat it over and over again. Drill it into your mind and make sure that you never forget why you're pushing towards those goals. If you keep it in the front of your mind, you won't lose sight of it. You'll keep on pushing until you reach your goals.

If you can't find a strong enough reason why you want to achieve your goals, then they aren't important enough for you to achieve. You have to spend the time and actually write this out. Just like painting the financial picture, this is just as important to the success of your financial goals. Find a strong enough reason why. Dig deep. Dig as deep as you humanly can. Search deep within your heart and your spirit, and then write it out. Actually write it out on paper, or type it out. When you do this, feel the emotion of the reason. Feel the severity of the reasons why you must achieve your goal. This isn't about how you *should* achieve it; it's about how you *must* achieve it.

CREATING A BUDGET

After you've laid out your financial picture for yourself, set your financial goals, and you have a clear understanding of just where you stand versus where you want to be, it's time to create a budget. If you've never created a budget in the past, then it's time to do so now. By having a budget, it will help you stay on track financially and avoid being derailed, time and time again. Your financial picture is a good starting point for your budget. You know just how much money you need once you've whittled your way down to the bare essentials. Once you've trimmed off the excess expenses in your life, you know just how much money you can spend, and just how much you can put towards paying down that debt, saving, and investing.

The good news is that, today, there are a lot of tools that exist, from phone and tablet apps, to online software, which allow you to help track your spending and your debt. You can use these automated tools to help you track and keep a budget. It's okay to use a resource such as this, or use the trusty old way of pen and paper by keeping meticulous notes. But, if you have a hard time tracking your expenses on pen and paper, use a smartphone app, or create a budget on your computer using a spreadsheet. The important thing here is to track every penny that you spend. This is critical to seeing where the money is going every month.

To create a budget, you have to understand just how much money you have to work with each month. Your budget will be your income minus your fixed expenses. Now, you still have your variable expenses to deal with, but your budget should take into account how much money is going towards variable expenses. Once you know just how much money you have to work with, it's time to start prioritizing. Create a separate list, which details all of the categories of spending you partake in on a monthly basis. Whether it's your cable bill, your electricity bill, your groceries, and so on, list these all down, but start with the most important one at the top. When you prioritize your budget like this, you can ensure that the most important expenses will get covered. Work your way down to the least important expenses, and ensure you leave some left over to invest in your rainy day fund.

You should also keep in mind that you could always call your creditors to negotiate down your interest rates. If you have revolving debt payments on credit cards with high rates, and you have an excellent payment history, credit card companies will be willing to work with you on the interest rate. If not, see if you can find a low-interest rate card that you can transfer your balance to. But, the goal is, once you transfer that debt, you have to pay down as much as you can. Don't ignore it just because it's switched to a zero percent interest rate for a short period of time. It won't stay at a low rate forever, and the more you can do to tackle the principal balance, the better off you will be later down the road when a higher rate kicks in.

You'll be surprised at just how willing revolving debt

payment companies will be to work with you on your interest rates. If you call them and explain your situation, and tell them you're trying to pay off the debt, someone will likely help you. You may have to deal with a few customer service reps that may not be as helpful, but there's always that one who you'll get from time to time, who will be compassionate and caring enough to assist you with your plans to tackle your debt. Don't give up and don't stop trying. If you've missed some payments, find out how many you need to make in a row until you can renegotiate your rate, then make the payments, and set a calendar date to call back to lower the rates. The better organized you are, the easier the process will be for you.

The worst thing that you can possibly do is to do nothing. If you don't paint your financial picture, set goals, create a budget, and tackle your debt, you won't be any better off one, two, three, and even ten years down the road. I know that it's hard at times to see past the immediate blockades you may have standing before you and your goals, but I assure you that with a little bit of time, you'll get through it. As long as you don't give up and throw in that towel, you'll plow through it eventually. Remember that nothing worth achieving is going to be easy; nothing. Stick to it, push through, and you'll persevere. Eventually, you'll get closer and closer to your goal, until one day you'll make that major breakthrough. But, you have to start somewhere. You have to start now.

3

YOUR FINANCIAL HARDWIRING

"Your net worth to the world is usually determined by what remains after your bad habits are subtracted from your good ones." – *Benjamin Franklin*

Peter sat in the restaurant booth with his closest friend and business partner, James. The conversation was a serious one. They were in dire financial straits and their business was failing. In an effort to determine whether they should let the ship sink, or hang on and fight the good fight, they decided to hash it out over dinner at their favorite restaurant.

The two long time friends were about as opposite as two people could get. Peter was the wild risk taker of the two, while James was the steadfast one who was always crunching the numbers and warning of perilous doom if they continued the same course. James tried to steer the business in the right direction, but it was of no use. Peter was bringing them both down.

James was initially reluctant to enter into business with Peter. He knew how eager his state-of-mind could be at times, and in James' eyes, Peter exhibited irrational exuberance. But, he held onto the fact that, as entrepreneurs, eagerness can go a long way. He held onto the fact that, just maybe, he and his long-time friend could make that business a success. And, Peter had always looked up to James. Although they were high school pals, James had achieved significant success in business, while Peter was still struggling. Eager to make his mark on the world, Peter was able to convince James to go into business together, something James later regretted.

"So what do we do now?" Peter asked. He looked at James with hope and mild aspirations to see things through. "I really want to make this work. Don't you think we can make this work?"

James looked at his friend with remorse. "No, Peter, we can't. Look at where we've come to. Look at the financial picture that I've just painted for you. Look at these numbers," he said, pointing to the piece of paper James had drawn out for the both of them on the table. He had carefully outlined just how much debt and expenses the business was carrying, and how low the income numbers were in comparison.

"I understand but I still think we can make it work."

"How? Tell me how? We've had this conversation numerous times. We've been down this road before. You always make promises that you're going to pull your weight, but all I get from you is slack. You're bringing down this ship, Peter, and I can't do this on my own anymore. I'm throwing away my hard-earned money at this thing, and it's sinking. Peter, it's sinking fast."

"I know," said Peter. He looked down at the table at the piece of paper that showed the financial hole they had dug for themselves. *What happened? What went wrong?* "I don't understand, I thought we planned well for this whole thing, but I guess I just miscalculated. I don't know. Maybe I just wasn't paying enough attention."

James looked at him now with disdain. "Not paying enough attention? That's what I've been saying this whole time!" James was furious.

"Please, don't raise your voice. Not here," Peter said.

"Seriously? That's what you care about right now? I don't understand you. You said you were going to take this business seriously. That was the only reason why I threw myself at this thing with you. But, all I've seen is someone who wants to have fun. Life isn't a party Peter, and you can't piss away all of our money by spending it frivolously on marketing efforts that don't ever pan out. You have to run the numbers. You have to be more careful. This isn't a game. It's a business. How come it's taking you so long to come to that realization?"

James was well within his rights to be furious, he had put up with Peter's nonchalant attitude towards the business for far too long. Mistake after mistake, Peter had pushed them to the brink of financial ruin. The worst part was that he was taking his friend down with him, a friend who had worked so hard and toiled so tirelessly to help make their business a success, but Peter ruined it. He ruined it because he had been selfish. He ruined it because he hadn't paid attention to the details.

"I'm sorry, James. Really, I'm sorry." Peter looked down at the table, and all he could see was red. He didn't understand where he went wrong. He didn't understand why he never listened to that voice inside of his head telling him he needed to clean up his act. "I think I need help, Peter. I don't know what else to do."

"Stop feeling sorry for yourself. This isn't about you anymore. This is about us. You should have paid attention more; you should have listened when I put up the warning signs. Do you think this was all some big game?"

James was furious. Peter didn't understand the severity of the situation. He had had the same conversation with him numerous times over, but he still wasn't getting it.

"I know, Jim, but... I guess what I'm trying to say is... I don't know where I went wrong. I don't know why I dragged us down into this situation."

"It's bad, Peter. It's really bad. There's no saving this company now. We really are in a bad situation. I'm not willing to stick my neck out on the line here anymore. I really don't see this going anywhere good anytime soon. This ship is about to run aground, Peter. I'm telling you this is bad."

"Let me try to figure it out," said Peter. "I know there has to be a solution. There just has to be."

"You keep saying that, but then you keep ignoring the problems that exist right in front of your nose. You're either too ignorant or too stupid. Look... I know our friendship goes back a long time, but this is more than about being friends. This is business, Peter, and we said we would always be honest and forthright with one another when it came to business. This is how I feel, and to be honest, I can't continue to bleed money like this anymore."

The waitress came with the check just as they were having their spat, and she was sorry she interrupted them. They both looked at her as though she were the last person on earth they wanted to see. She dropped the check, and scurried quickly away.

"I'll get this," Peter said.

"No, I'll get it, but this is the last time, Peter. This is the last time that I'm going to be paying for anything that has to do with this business or us. I'm through. This is no way to run a company. You should be ashamed of yourself."

James threw down the cash and left. Peter looked down at it with disdain. He hated that he had allowed money to get the best of him. He hated that he had dipped into the company's funds in order to fuel his own lifestyle. He hated all of it. Most of all he hated himself. He had gone behind the back of one of his best and only friends.

What are you going to do now, Peter? What are you going to do now?

*****

Money can make you do things you never once thought you could do. It has this strange power and mystique. Once humble men and women, become empowered when money comes into their hands. They feel unstoppable, like they can do anything. That is, until the stream of money runs dry. And, all too often, we don't take the time to properly calculate the flowing of that stream of money. We don't look at what's flowing downstream and upstream. We fail to pay attention to debt and expenses at key points in time, and we begin to self-sabotage.

Depending on your experiences in life, and the current status of your psychic apparatus, you have your own way of behaving around money. When money flows through your hands, you might feel a certain sense of elation. Whether we like it or not, money is an emotionally-charged subject, and depending on your unique subconscious configuration, you'll respond just a little bit differently when it comes to money than the next person will. This is all part of your financial schematic, which has been hardwired into your mind as you've come of age. Money is ingrained into your sense of self, and your attachment to money will be purely unique and different than it will be for the next person.

In the previous chapters, we saw that within our psyche, there exists a three-component structural model that controls our behavior. This psychic apparatus is at the very heart of our decision-making process. When we're contemplating a decision, our psychic apparatus is weighing the pros and cons of that decision against the predominant forces of the id, ego, and superego. We base our final decision, or behavior, on a multitude of different factors. But, how are the dominant forces formed in your psyche? How is that one person can be so responsible when it comes to money and saving, and another person cannot?

The discussion goes back to why we do the things that we do. There's always a reason for our behavior. Somewhere, deep down inside, there's a reason that we overspend, overeat, or overindulge in whatever it may be. We're trying to fulfill some need or void, and in our complex minds, our actions are pushing us towards fulfilling that in some way. If you take the alcoholic for example, who knows that they drink too much, yet still does it anyway, they too are fulfilling a need. To them, alcohol brings pleasure in the short term, and the brain has been hardwired to receive that pleasure. Not receiving that pleasure would mean immense amounts of pain. The mind thinks it's helping that person to avoid pain, when really it's prolonging it and making it worse.

But, when it comes down to a conversation about you

and your finances, when you take a clear look at why you do the things that you do, you'll see that your mind is simply trying to fill a need. It's trying to gain pleasure while avoiding pain. If you've ever waited until the last minute to file your taxes for example, your mind, until that last moment, was avoiding pain and gaining pleasure. But, when the pain of not filing your taxes exceeded the pleasure of ignoring it, the scales tipped. This happens when the deadline approaches and you realize that it's going to mean a lot more pain if you don't file your taxes, than if you simply just get it done.

Your ability to control your finances stems from your emotions, and those emotions stem from your psychic apparatus developed during your rearing as a child. Based on your upbringing, your predominant forces in your psychic apparatus will be unique to you. It will interpret social and environmental cues in a unique way that passes through the filter of your own life's experiences. These all combine to create a financial hardwiring. That financial hardwiring is your money schematic, or in essence, your financial blueprint. It determines the way in which you see money decisions, and without understanding and building awareness towards your financial hardwiring, money will continue to control you.

The financial hardwiring is part of the overall hardwiring of our psychic apparatus that develops in its majority during our first five years on this earth. That hardwiring fuses a certain basic programming into our minds. It creates a set of operating rules and commands for which we interpret life's experiences from that point on. As we have more and more experiences, that hardwiring becomes more set in place over time. And, although the hardwiring can change, without a specific awareness towards your own way of operating, modifying your approach and behavior becomes incredibly difficult. Why? Because the hardwiring is part of whom we are; it's

part of the identification with our selves. It's the ego's way
of giving itself an identity. When you try to change the
hardwiring, there's always a system malfunction because
something that has been so commonplace, begins to get
uprooted.

This is why it's so difficult for most people to change
behavior, which is rooted in their hardwiring. When you've
grown up to interpret experiences in a certain way, it's hard
to see things differently. Think about extremists in any
light for instance. You have political extremists, religious
extremists, environment extremists, and so on. Those
people have a certain hardwiring that's virtually impossible
to change. That's because they compounded all of their
experiences and filtered them through their psyche, which
further reinforced their hardwiring. Whether it's a religious
hardwiring, financial hardwiring, or any other type, it's
virtually set in stone. But, it doesn't have to be that way;
people can change if they want to bad enough.

PSYCHOSEXUAL STAGES

The origins of our actions stem from our upbringings. As we grow and mature, we have a certain authority element in our lives. Whether the authority comes from our parents, our guardians, our mentors, or anyone else for that matter, some form of authority exists in our lives. How each person handles authority, or succumbs to the authority in their life, has a major impact on their financial hardwiring. This is because your financial hardwiring is a partial imprint of your psychic apparatus. If you could think of circuits on a computer's motherboard for a moment as your financial hardwiring, then the microchips and transistors on the board would be your experiences. Those experiences fuse onto the mind's motherboard, and they help to determine the dominant forces in a person's psychic apparatus.

Our psychic apparatus molds and shapes itself based on our experiences. This all occurs in our lives by the time we reach the age of five-years-old, after we've completed what's called the psychosexual stages. The personality forms through three primary psychosexual stages. During these first five years of personality development, the id breaks off to form the ego and the superego. These are the most important stages during the development of the human mind. And, as we pass through from one stage to the next, we must resolve conflict within our own minds. If the conflict isn't resolved, we can't move onto the next stage in a successful transition.

During the first five years of development, children raised in a very tumultuous home, have trouble as adults. The mind's development, and financial hardwiring, is all dependent on these first stages of development. The problem is that, it's very difficult to recall these first five years of your life without the aid of information from a parent or guardian, whose opinions may not always be the straight facts. Each parent has a certain way of raising their children; ways that may not be socially acceptable, so determining your true experiences are difficult unless you know the specific truth.

Some people have difficulty leaving one of these stages in their lives because either they didn't meet their adequate needs in the stage, or they were more than adequately met in a certain stage and were reluctant to move onto the next. This causes either frustration or overindulgence later on in life and either one of these – or a combination of the two – can lead to the fixation on a particular psychosexual stage where a person permanently invests a small portion of their libido in that specific stage of psychosexual development.

Oral Stage (0 – 1 years)

The first stage of psychosexual development is the oral stage, where the libido finds its center in a baby's mouth. This is where the id is strongest at first, and in order to satisfy the demands of the id at this stage, there's a focus on mouth-oriented activities such as breast-feeding, biting, and sucking. Excessive oral stimulation at this stage in development could lead to an oral fixation in later stages in life, especially during times of high stress. We see oral fixations translated in adults through people who excessively smoke, or bite and chew on their nails. Their fixation remains at the oral stage of development in life, and this transmutes itself into adult fixations.

Anal Stage (1 – 3 years)

During this psychosexual stage in life, we become aware of the anus, and as children, we begin to derive pleasure from the act of defecating. This is the stage where the id breaks off and develops into the ego, and superego, because the child becomes aware that their wishes aren't always aligned with their parents' wishes. Meaning, they can't defecate wherever they choose to once their parents remove their diapers. During the diaper stage, children defecate on demand, so there's no authority there that's blocking them or preventing them from doing so.

This stage of development is extremely important to your financial hardwiring, because depending on how severely you were potty trained, you will derive pleasure from either spending lots of money, or saving it. In essence, this stage also determines a child's view on all authority in their lives. If for example the child is potty trained very harshly, or with severe measures, they tend to be very anal-retentive. They hold onto their money – just as their parents taught them to hold onto their poo – they're very tidy, and they hate messes. They will excessively clean, save, and ensure that things are in proper order in their lives.

The main reason that this occurs is because when a child is potty trained in this excessive manner, they begin to gain pleasure from holding onto their feces. As strange as this may sound, the truth of the matter is that, this leads to a major impact on the financial hardwiring of a child, and the adult that he or she becomes. When a parent then insists that a child defecate by placing them on the toilet, they create an authority relationship that ingrains this type of behavior. It makes the person very organized mentally.

On the other hand, however, if a child isn't properly potty trained during this stage, the opposite happens. This psychosexual stage plays a major role in our financial hardwiring, because this is where the id breaks off to form the ego, and superego. When the child isn't potty trained, and is allowed to roam more freely, without as much insistence from authority, they become excessive spenders, more messy, and disorganized. This also leads to a more rebellious spirit and the desire to always share their thoughts, and their feelings with you, in a very liberal manner.

Try to think back if you can to this stage in your life. You most likely won't be able to recall it all on your own, but with the help of a parent or guardian, you can determine how they reared you. This has an important impact on your financial hardwiring. How they raised you, and just how quickly you succumbed to authority, plays a major role in how you spend and save your money. As outlandish as this may seem at first, it's a very eye-opening experience to find out just how much this psychosexual stage aligns with how you are today. Knowing this also serves to help you realize that a lot of your behavior was out of your control. Until now, you were unaware of how your past was affecting your present. Obviously there are many more layers, which have been laid down within your personality through the filter of your experiences, but the base layer in this psychosexual stage is one of the most important ones.

Phallic Stage (3 – 5 years)

The most important stage of psychosexual development is the phallic stage. This is the stage where the child begins to associate the libido with his or her genitals. This is also the stage where feelings like jealousy and resentment form, along with attraction and fear. In boys, Freud called this the Oedipus complex and the Electra complex in girls. The conflict in this stage is resolved only when the child begins to adapt the same characteristics of the parent of the same sex. So, this means if you're a male, many of your characteristics stem from your father originally, and if you're a female, from your mother. This doesn't mean that you're a carbon copy of them; it just means that you took on many of their characteristics.

There is a lot of copying and imitating that goes on in this psychosexual stage where the child begins to mimic the characteristics of the same sex parent to move past the conflict of the Oedipus complex or the Electra complex. There's an association here that becomes a very strong one, and the child takes on the same sex parent's characteristics as part of their financial hardwiring. If you're a woman, and your mother was very thrifty and conservative, then you'll have similar characteristics. If you're a man and your father was liberal with his money, and an excessive spender, you'll usually also adopt these traits.

Think about it for a moment. What are your parents' views on money? How does your same sex parent spend his or her money? Are they frugal? Are they liberal in their spending? Did they try to raise you to be identical to them or different? Maybe they made some mistakes in life, and tried to instill a different set of morals in you. Maybe they failed because you simply copied what you saw. It's important because of the major effect this is having on your life. When you can recognize where your behavior stems from, you can build more awareness to it. Building awareness is the first step to fixing the problems that may have resulted in your life.

Of course, just understanding your past isn't the answer to the millionaire method. This is only part of the answer. This is just a crucial part of the answer as is painting your financial picture, setting your goals, and taking action towards them. But the past also helps to shed light on the present. If you don't want to continue repeating the same mistakes of the past, use the experiences you learn to help support and empower you to make the right choices in the future. Use the honest awareness towards enlightening your future, not dimming it.

FINANCIAL HARDWIRING

A person's financial hardwiring, then, is a combination of very many factors. During the psychosexual stages, when we begin to develop the ego and superego, we are acutely aware of any sayings that our same sex parent says. If your same sex parent always said money doesn't grow on trees, then there may be a scarcity factor in your life. You may look at money as if there is never enough of it. You may act in accordance with this scarcity mentality, which breeds more scarcity. Thoughts are very powerful in this aspect, and this can have a severe impact on your financial capacity. When you live in scarcity and lack, it's very difficult to push past this into the area of abundance.

For most people, this isn't something they can control because it occurred during personality development. It's something that's ingrained in us, and that we identify with. In fact, that's the purpose of the phallic stage of psychosexual development – for identification. We identify with the self in this stage and begin to take on a sense of characteristics and traits, which is why this developmental phase is so impactful. It can literally define every other part

95

of your behavior because it creates a set of beliefs for you to live by. When you hear something like money doesn't grow on trees, it becomes a belief. For most people, beliefs are like truths, and it's very difficult to sway them otherwise. Just think of some of the strong beliefs held by people in politics, religion, gun control, abortion, or any other area in life. Beliefs can be powerful, very powerful.

On the other hand, if your same sex parent always said money is no object, then you may have a tendency to overspend. Just like the parent saying that money doesn't grow on trees, the ones that say money is no object, also have a significant impact on our lives. When we hear a powerful statement like that, we are setup for a feeling of abundance, as if there will always be more around the corner. However, without the right checks and balances, this can also lead to a detrimental decline as a person spends and spends, until they have nothing more to spend. And, getting into a high debt situation like this can be brutal and very difficult to climb out of. If you've had some experience with debt in the past, then you know exactly what I mean.

The hard part about this is that we adopt these characteristics when growing up, and these traits are very difficult to shake. They become so habitually ingrained in our financial hardwiring that changing our viewpoint becomes difficult. However, change is possible. Changing your financial hardwiring is possible by first building awareness towards it. Just like with painting your financial picture, by being honest and aware of your behavior, you can make strides to change it. This really is at the basis of who you are and why you do the things that you do.

UNCOVERING YOUR FINANCIAL HARDWIRING

To really build awareness towards your beliefs, you'll need to pull out another sheet of paper. And, you'll have to think back for a moment. Think back to the time when you were young and much influenced by your parents. Think back to the things your same sex parent or guardian said. Think about the words they uttered in your household. What comes to mind? What sayings stick out for you that you heard repeated over, and over again? We all have them in our mind. We all have those sayings that we always go back to; they're our defaults. They are like home to us, and make us feel comfortable.

These truths, so to speak, are the foundational building blocks that we've used to erect the personalities and traits of our lives. They are the characteristics installed on top of those beliefs, which have formed our identities. Think back to your childhood now and try to recall things that were said as a child by your same sex parent. Usually, those same words and patterns repeated themselves throughout your childhood, so you don't necessarily have to remember back to when you were three to five years of age. You could also ask your same sex parent, if possible, what types of things he or she said to you as a child. They may not have been acutely aware of what they were saying themselves, but by digging and asking others such as relatives, you may be able to find the answers.

This awareness to your financial hardwiring is critical to the millionaire method, because without changing this hardwiring, you can't change your thoughts and approach to money. You will always look at money in a way that will limit you, because we are all a product of our own experiences that have shaped our lives. You will always automatically go back, through subconscious behavior, to your mind's conditioning as a child. But, the majority of that viewpoint was developed at such an early age that it's difficult to spot unless you know what to look for. It's important to come to this awareness if you're going to work to change your financial hardwiring.

Write down on a sheet of paper all of those sayings that you can think of. Did your same sex parent say money is the root of all evil? Or, maybe he or she said, work hard, go to school, and you'll get a good job. Or maybe it was, penny-wise, pound-foolish. Whatever they said, write it down. Act like a detective to uncover the past because these are the beliefs that have created you. Your financial hardwiring is laden with these beliefs. And, try to go back and recall everything you can in your childhood as it related to money. What experiences and beliefs stick out the most?

This detective work will help you uncover your financial hardwiring, and expose it. The most important aspect here is that when you uncover and expose this, your ego can't hide behind it anymore, because you've built awareness to it. Remember the push and pull between the id, ego, and superego? Well, the ego likes to shroud a lot of its behavior in the fact that you don't have all the information. When you hide from your beliefs, and the facts, the ego can do a lot of maneuvering, allowing the id to get its way. When you uncover the facts, expose them, and build awareness, the ego has nowhere to hide. This is why these exercises are so important.

For example, let's take the abuser of alcohol. This individual has severe substance dependence. He or she is reliant on alcohol because they've set up in their mind that it brings them a great deal of pleasure. It brings them pleasure in the short term, because they know that as soon as they place that bottle or glass to their lips, they have a sense of relief. Their cares and their worries seem to disappear into thin air, and they suddenly feel like they can do anything, go anywhere, and accomplish anything. But, they're numbing the true emotions that are hidden and buried deep down inside. That's what alcohol does to the alcoholic; it acts as an escape. Alcohol is their escape from caring about all the worries that are weighing them down; worries that are buried deep down inside. But, when an alcoholic hits rock bottom, they learn to rebuild their personalities by digging deep into their past and building awareness to the things that drove them into that behavior. Overspending, overeating, and just about any other indulgence is all the same. You must look to the past in order to uncover what's limiting you in the present.

Internal conflict creates a massive weight in our minds, which we're busy grappling with in our subconscious. When you can't deal with uncovering issues from the past, they will result in problems in the future. And, alcohol is only one such popular drug of choice that helps to mask those issues because it's easy to consume, easy to obtain, and it's cheap. It doesn't take a lot of money to get drunk and stay drunk, and when the money runs out, the alcoholic has to improvise by turning to elicit activities to continue the emotion-numbing behavior. Similarly, when a person overspends, they're essentially doing the same thing. Their drug of choice is money, but the problem is that once the money runs out, they face the same situation. They can no longer engage in the emotion-numbing activity. They usually find another emotion-numbing activity. But, all of these are really covering up those issues that haven't been dealt with. They're covering up the issues that have yet to be faced.

So, by taking the time to write out your recollections of your childhood, you can work towards uncovering your financial hardwiring. Sit down with your same sex parent, or call them on the phone and quiz them. Quiz them about your past, and ask them questions about how they raised you. If you can't remember everything, just ask. Ask them about your potty training, and ask them about whether you were breast-fed, and for how long. Ask them how strict they were, and then go into uncovering what they said about money. How did they look at money growing up? Ask your same sex parent how they felt about money when they were your age. This will help to uncover many of your own characteristics, because you're a spitting image of your same sex parent, like it or not.

By building this awareness, you can take the first step in uncovering your financial hardwiring. The difficulty is being honest enough with yourself to realize why you do the things you do. Why do you overspend? What emotions or internal conflicts are you trying to mask? What are you unhappy about? What about your life is bothering you? Usually, these are signs of other, larger problems that you still need to deal with. This is all critical because the millionaire method requires a certain mental fortitude, and approach. The millionaire method requires a quiet, strong, powerful, and committed approach that doesn't falter. When you have hidden internal conflicts that you numb by engaging in certain activities that may or may not include overspending, overeating, overdrinking, and any other related behavior, it will truly limit you. It will limit you from achieving the life of your dreams.

REWIRING YOUR FINANCIAL HARDWIRING

Once you've uncovered your financial hardwiring, and you have a better glimpse into your own personal development, you are that much closer to embracing the millionaire method. However, the hard part with the financial hardwiring is the rewiring. You have to rewire your financial thinking and completely throw out the old behaviors and habits that weren't serving you. You have to replace them with new behaviors, thoughts, and habits that will serve you. But, just like with losing weight, quitting smoking, or getting out of debt, it will take time. Habits are formed after six months of consistent behavior, so don't expect to have a new habit form overnight. The millionaire method is about the long-term commitment to a plan of action, and a way of thinking. It's about trying to suppress the urges of the ego and id, and replace them with a much more logical and calculated decision-making process.

To rewire your thinking and behavior, you have to look at your present thinking and behavior. Once you understand your present behavior, you can work on replacing these thoughts and limiting beliefs with new ones that will help to serve you. The millionaire method of thinking should work to empower you, not hold you back. If you keep the same mentality that you've always had, and just try to work harder, you will always fall back into the same patterns. This is why it's so difficult for alcoholics to quit drinking, smokers to stop smoking, and habitual drug users to stop using. It's so hard because these have become habits developed over years and years. It's something that's comfortable to them, because they are all emotion-numbing activities. They all help to mask the true hidden emotions buried deep down inside.

We all do this at some point in our lives. We all have a tendency to want to escape from our obligations. We want to jet off and run away to some far off place, or lay on some exotic island in the middle of nowhere. That's because most of us are unhappy. We're unhappy with the way things are in our lives, so we try to implement ways to escape and numb the emotions. We don't want to have to think about things that are bothering us. But, that's the design of our psyches in general. If you can't master these emotions, and become aware of your limiting behavior, you can't embrace the millionaire method. For some people, this is a hard pill to swallow because the ego doesn't want you to believe that this is the case. The ego wants to keep the truth hidden from you. But, if it hasn't served you until now, then do something about it. Really dig deep and do something about it.

So, let's just say for example that your past thoughts and financial hardwiring revolved around the scarcity of money. Let's say your same sex parent always said money doesn't buy happiness. By saying something like this, it sets you up for a life where your relationship with money becomes a love hate one. You want money, but you hate it for some reason. Because, when you hear something like money doesn't buy happiness, and you've worked hard but found yourself deeper in debt, you begin to loath money. You begin to loath it so much that your mind skews the concept of money. You know that you need money to survive, but you create a mental blockade for not wanting more than you actually need to get by. So, you have to change your thought patterns. You have to interrupt the old limiting beliefs and replace it with a new one that will serve you.

So let's say you want to replace the old thought of money doesn't buy happiness. We have to interrupt it and make fun of it so that you hear the new thought in your mind. You want to be able to picture something different when you hear the phrase, so you can change the saying to money doesn't buy happiness, but it sure allows you to arrive at your problems in style. Can you see how this is a fun way of poking at an old saying? See if you can come up with some creative sayings to rethink your old limiting thoughts. Spend as much time on this as you need. This is important. This is just as important as painting your overall financial picture, and just as important as setting your financial goals as well. Because the root cause of your situation rests in the psychology of your mind, and that's something many people don't choose to tackle.

By rewiring some of the old sayings you've heard growing up as a child, you can begin on the pathway to fixing some of your behavior when it comes to money. The problem is that in school we get a formal education. However, that formal education isn't a financial education, so what we hear at home about money highly influences us. In school we learn to study hard, get good grades, and then get a steady job. But, the problem is that, in between, there's so much noise. There are so many distractions along the way, and our personalities are so very vulnerable to these distractions. We don't receive a financial education that dives into the psychology of why we do the things we do. That psychology is what limits our behavior and holds us back.

Separate your sheet of paper into two separate columns. On that paper, write the old saying, and write down the ways in which you lived your life according to this old belief that's ingrained in your mind. Then, on the right side, rework the belief. Rework it so that it serves you. Poke fun at it if you have to, but do this exercise. After you reword the old belief, write down the reasons why you'll live by the new belief from now on. Go back to your financial goals to look at the reasons why you wanted to achieve those goals. Reference those reasons why, and write down reasons why you must live by the new beliefs. Write down why you must rewire your financial hardwiring.

Keep these new beliefs with you, and each month, come back to them when you repaint your financial picture and reset your goals. Don't have New Year Syndrome when it comes to doing this work. Don't do it once and then forget about it for the rest of the year. To embody the millionaire method, you have to constantly assess and reassess your progress. See where you are every week and month. Soon, you'll get so used to this process that you'll do it every day. I look at my financial goals and beliefs on a daily basis, and I make sure that I'm living my life according to the beliefs that I set for myself long ago. You should do the same. Always assess and reassess, that's how you succeed at anything; that's how you rewire your financial hardwiring.

The problem is that it's easy to ignore hidden beliefs and debt when you choose not to look at it. When you tuck it under a rug and push it away, your ego can do a lot to help serve itself in these situations. Don't allow this to happen. Don't allow your ego to run your life in this manner. Make sure that you do each of these exercises, and you put your heart into it. Don't just do it for the sake of doing it; do it because it matters. It matters because it's your future on the line. It's so important to manifesting a bigger and brighter future for yourself and your family. Realize how important your financial hardwiring is, and work on rewiring it. At first, it will be hard because you're exposing the truth that your ego doesn't want you to see. But, eventually it will get easier to see; the ego will shrink as you become empowered with the truth.

If you can think back to anything that you overcame in the past, think about how you built awareness to where you were, versus where you wanted to be. It makes all the difference, and assessing and reassessing it is critical. You must constantly see where you are, versus where you want to be. You must always do this; it's one of the most important parts of the process. It's one of the most important parts of the millionaire method.

4
THE EMOTIONAL ROLLERCOASTER OF LIFE

"Your intellect may be confused, but your emotions will never lie to you." – Roger Ebert

Many people have trouble uncovering their true feelings about something. Most of the time, their true personalities come out when they are under a great deal of stress or facing a grave amount of internal conflict. However, it's natural for us to experience this internal strife on a consistent basis when we don't deal with the underlying root causes of our problems. When we don't deal with the issues at the very heart of our lives, life derails; the train carriage that's your life lifts off the track and goes off course. The problem is that, there's no user manual for human beings. There's no guidebook specifically designed for your own personality, and one that's unique to you. There's no booklet to help you decipher and debug your own personal problems and issues when you don't choose to see what's in front of your eyes.

When you can't deal with the root issues buried in your past, dealing with what's in front of you is impossible. Old baggage leads to a constant set of emotional and financial setbacks that can keep you back, and hold you back for the rest of your life. But, with an ego working in overdrive to help you avoid pain and gain pleasure, it's no wonder we don't choose to see what's before us, or deal with the difficult issues at hand. It's much easier for us to engage in the emotion-numbing activities that put off dealing with the pain for just another day. Eventually those days stack up on one another, and they turn into weeks, months, years, and decades. Eventually, the pain buries itself so deep down inside, that uncovering it and dealing with it becomes virtually impossible. It becomes virtually impossible to put your life in order, let alone your financial life in order, when you can't deal with the past.

Look, we are all the result of a unique set of experiences, and a unique upbringing. Even in the case of identical twins, there are always personality differences, because we all have experiences that are just a little more unique than the next person's is. Even if two people are virtually identical in every other way, they have had a cumulative set of experiences that are different. They haven't all felt, thought, and experienced the exact same things. And, because each one of us is unique, we all have unique problems and unique personalities that are a result of the combination of many factors. Of course, our psychosexual stages have a big impact on our lives, but so do the experiences that shape our lives after these stages are complete. Those experiences, combined with our unique psychosexual development, make us who we are today.

This is all-important because it lays the groundwork for the millionaire method. Without tackling your past and learning to deal with your emotions and uncover your demons, you won't be able to progress in life. You might find yourself taking a step forward only to face two steps back. But, when you deal with your own personality traits, and you uncover why it is you do the things you do, then your chances of success skyrocket. When you learn to clean up the wreckage of your past, and keep your emotions and your thoughts at bay, your potential is limitless. There's a lot to say about building this kind of awareness for your inner self and why you do the things you do. And, by rewiring your financial hardwiring, you can make the strides to embodying the millionaire method.

But, the hard part remains – what if you can't uncover your true hidden beliefs? What if you can't see past all the hurt and pain, to the bottled up feelings deep inside of you, which may be limiting you? What happens then? Well, this is common. This is common in fact across the board, because people have difficulty seeing the truth in their selves. They have difficulty facing the facts that may be too hard to face. That's why people don't want to paint their financial picture. They don't want to know how much debt they have. That would result in too much pain. They don't want to find out because they would have to change everything about themselves. They would have to alter all their behaviors and patterns that have become habitual to them.

Uncovering and unearthing all of that past hurt and pain is central to climbing out of debt, and embodying the millionaire method, because without doing so, you can't move past it. It will limit you till the day that you die, and if you find yourself getting ahead in life, you'll find yourself falling back again into the same negative patterns and routines. When you find yourself riding one of life's highs, you'll find life cutting you back down again two steps further behind than you were before. And, for some people, when they fall, they fall hard. Repeatedly failing in this manner is frustrating, and these frustrations can stack up upon one another to cause limitless amounts of frustration, fear, and anxiety.

However, when you learn to harness your emotions, and you learn to use them to empower you rather than to limit you, then you can truly open the door to living in abundance. This is a precursor to implementing any tools to increase your finances, clean up your debt, and begin saving and investing for the future. All of those things are critical, but if you can't deal with the emotional rollercoaster that's your life, then you won't be able to move forward. You won't be able to take an honest look at yourself and your present situation, and make a plan for advancement. Trust me, I've been there. In the past, I used to be frustrated after trying one thing after another to succeed. I would find myself becoming very successful, only to later have life knock me back down again, because I didn't learn to deal with the problems that were the root cause of my negative and limiting behavior. I didn't deal with the negative thought patterns that were running rampant on my life. If you don't deal with these things, they will ruin you; it's only just a matter of time.

LEVERAGING YOUR EMOTIONS

So how do you go about dealing with your past, in order to open the doors for your future? How do you go about understanding your emotions so that they empower you rather than limit you? To do this you need to uncover some of your hidden beliefs that are buried deep down inside. You need to take a close look at what you believe in about life, people, money, and the world, and you need to ensure that those beliefs align with your goals. If your beliefs and your goals clash, then you'll find yourself at odds with yourself. You'll feel your id, superego, and ego really tearing you apart. Your inner conflict, strife, and aggression will compound upon itself until you reach the breaking point. So you have to learn to align your core beliefs – what you truly believe in – with your financial goals.

The best way to uncover your beliefs, and your true inner self-talk in your mind, is through your emotions. Your emotions are the body's language for thought. If you hear something, or say something in your mind, even in your subconscious mind, that is then translated into emotions. If you begin to feel feelings of fear and anxiety, then there's a reason for that. If it happens out of the blue, then the talk is most likely occurring in your subconscious mind. If all of a sudden, you feel an enormous sense of fear or anxiety, and you can't recall a single conscious thought that led you to those feelings, your subconscious was speaking. Your subconscious was speaking and you were listening. You may not have been listening consciously, but you were certainly listening subconsciously.

When this happens to you – when you begin to feel emotions out of the blue – you have to stop whatever you're doing. You have to stop what you're doing and begin to analyze that thought pattern. You have to retrace those thoughts to see where they originated. If you think hard enough about it, you can notice the stream of conscious thought that may have led you to feeling that way. You must stop yourself as soon as you feel these emotions and work to uncover the true source of the feelings. What are you afraid of really? What are you anxious about?

In the past, if you've faced situations that seemed insurmountable, especially when it came to your finances, how did you overcome them? Did you end up winning the battle in the end? Or, is the war still being waged? Whatever that answer may be, your emotions are what spur you to act the way you do in life. Your emotions are what signal you to take action without thinking about it. When we bubble up with feelings of anger and hatred, we lash out. We take action without even knowing it. Most people simply blow up, and unleash a terrible amount of fury that lay hidden inside of them, dormant.

Similarly, when it comes to finances, we act out in certain ways when we experience certain emotions. Usually, our actions work to mask the emotions of pain, guilt, fear, regret, and jealously. We use money as a tool to help us indulge in certain behavior that will hide the true emotions that we're trying to cover up. Money becomes a temporary Band-Aid used to cover up the true hurt that we don't want to experience or unleash. We don't want to because we're doing more to avoid pain than we are to gain pleasure. You have to recognize this, and you have to deal with the emotions as they come up. Realize that your ego doesn't control you. If you pay enough attention, and are aware, you can control it. You can suppress your id when you come to the realization that this is what it's trying to do.

No matter what types of emotions you feel, if they're negative ones, you have to work to build awareness and deal with the issues at the heart of them. If you don't master your emotions, they will master you. And, the millionaire method requires a mastery of your emotions, because without this tool, you can't arguably control your destiny because you'll be at the mercy of the whims of your psychic apparatus. You have to be able to control your emotions, and to do that you have to control your thoughts. Your thoughts are producing your emotions. Your subconscious stream of thought is taking you down the road of fear, anxiety, and anger. In order to control those emotions, you must deal with them, but at the heart of those emotions are your thoughts. Your thought patterns are really driving home those emotions.

THOUGHTS INTO EMOTIONS

Your thoughts are at the root of all that you are. You have anywhere from 50,000 to 60,000 thoughts that run through your mind on a daily basis. And, for many people, most of those thoughts are negative thoughts. They are fear-based thoughts that include nervousness, anxiety, resentment, guilt, and many other thoughts that don't serve them. These negative thoughts elicit negative emotions in the body. So, if one day you burst into an uncontrollable fit of tears, it's those subconscious thoughts that drove you there.

When you have beliefs buried deep down inside of you, which remain covered and secret, your ego can use those to control you. It can do what it wants to help shroud your true inner feelings from coming to light. It knows that as soon as those feelings come to light, it won't be able to hide anymore, but until they do, you'll continue experiencing huge amounts of internal conflict and strife. You must take control of your thoughts, so that you can take control of your emotions. If you can't control your thoughts, then you'll find yourself slipping back into old and destructive patterns that don't serve you. If you overspend your money on shopping, travel, or general entertainment, it's your thoughts that are feeding the emotions that drive that spending. It all starts in the mind, and if you're going to have a millionaire mentality, you have to eradicate the negative thoughts from your mind.

The key to doing this is creating new affirmations. Affirmations are statements that you repeat over and over again, until you mind accepts them as truths. Since everything in this world is merely a construct of our minds, building an affirmative set of thoughts that's repeated over, and over again, can literally change the course of your life. This doesn't mean you get to ignore your problems; it means that you have to replace your negative patterns of thinking, with positive ones. Negative thoughts won't get you anywhere, which is why you always hear the saying the rich get richer, and the poor get poorer. It's because like begets like. Rich experiences build onto rich thoughts, and poor experiences build onto poor thoughts. Both types of individuals have a certain set of beliefs, experiences, and thoughts that create the foundation of their viewpoints. If you want to override those thoughts that are filtered by your beliefs, change your thoughts and your beliefs, then build up new experiences to support them.

This won't happen overnight. The millionaire method isn't about an overnight success, or hitting the jackpot with some get-rich-quick scheme. This is about modifying thoughts and behavior to empower you, rather than to limit you. If you can't get down to the root of what's driving your behavior, then you can't make significant strides to repair yourself. Work on replacing those limiting thoughts with ones that are empowering, and it will change your entire perspective on your finances and your life in general.

LEARNING TO CONTROL YOUR EMOTIONS

It's clear that emotions don't appear out of nowhere. They don't just show up out of thin air just to make your life more difficult. No, your emotions stem from your own mind, and those thoughts running through it. Those 50,000 or so thoughts that run through your mind are evoking those emotions. They're stoking the fire of feelings by running through every fiber of your body. Learning to manage these emotions as they occur is one of the biggest tools in the arsenal of the millionaire method. While this may not sound as important to you as more money in the bank, it is remarkably so. That's because without the underlying psychological tools to help control and understand your behavior, you'll be at the mercy of your subconscious thoughts and emotions.

To recognize your negative thoughts, you have to pay careful attention. Sit still for fifteen minutes; turn off all distractions including your phone, the Internet, and anything else that can interrupt you. Just sit there in silence and close your eyes. Your mind will eventually wander off and when it does, you have to catch it; catch what it's thinking about as soon as you begin feeling some powerful emotions. What is it saying? What are the negative patterns it's running? For most people, these are fears and anxieties – life's what-ifs. If you can be completely aware of this talk in your mind, then you can eliminate it. If you don't control your thoughts, then they're going to control you. And, those thoughts will produce emotions that will force you to take actions that have become habitual to you. Nothing will change if you can't control your thoughts. You'll find yourself going back out and overspending again, even after you've worked so hard to change things for the better. Don't slip back into old, negative patterns. Take control of your thoughts, your emotions, and your life.

This exercise requires careful patience, a calming of the mind, and the noises inside your head. Eventually, the mind begins to wander off, and when it does, you have to catch those thoughts dead in their tracks. Write down what you said in your mind. See if you can trace those thoughts back to where they stemmed from. Write it out on a piece of paper, and trace the thought patterns. Your thoughts run through the filter of your beliefs and your experiences. Two different people will have two very different thoughts based upon those beliefs and experiences. If you really want to control your financial destiny, you have to control your thoughts. Replace the negative thoughts with positive ones.

When you feel a negative emotion come up, and you're able to see it or feel it, stop what you're doing. When you feel a negative emotion, it's a signal that your body is thinking fear-based or anxiety-based thoughts. You may not have been conscious of the thoughts when they occurred, but try to retrace its steps. Where did the stream of subconscious thought start? If you're feeling fearful of something, why are you afraid? What's the worst that can happen?

When it comes to money, fear is one of the most debilitating factors that will work against you in succeeding with the millionaire method. Fear can limit you, break you, second-guess you, and destroy you financially. It can cripple you to the point where you can't act because you're too afraid of the consequences. Either it's the fear of investing your money, fear of not being able to enjoy life and have enough money to spend, fear of paying too much money in taxes, or whatever it may be. Fear and anxiety are severely crippling when it comes to your finances.

If you feel the fear when it comes to money or your future nest egg, remove yourself from the situation that you're in immediately. Take a moment and go get some fresh air, or grab a pen and paper and begin writing out your thoughts. Write out why you're afraid and try to react the opposite of how you would normally react. If you normally lose your temper, or begin to get agitated, do something to avoid that. Hit the gym, go for a run, or do some other stress-releasing activity. If you can interrupt the pattern and look at why you're so fearful in the first place, you can work on correcting the problem.

Finally, think about your choices logically. If situations confront you where your emotions begin to take over, stop and really analyze that, and analyze how you want to react. If you're very susceptible to spending money in certain situations, realize that and do something about it. Fix the problem by not putting yourself into those situations. If you spend too much money at the bar, or by going out for meals too often, then cut up your credit cards. Whatever you need to do, make sure that you make a logical and conscious decision, and don't allow your thoughts and your emotions to control you. Learn to control them.

By taking control of your emotions, you can take

control of your financial future. We can talk all we want about how and where to invest your money, how to generate more income, but none of that will help you if you can't get control of the driver of the ship. If you can't steer your mind in the right direction, even if you make good choices from time to time, you might end up jumping ship later on. When people get too comfortable, they begin to make poor decisions. And, it's very easy to slip into this, believe me; I'm speaking from experience. But, as you make mistakes, you must learn from them. Don't repeat the mistakes of your past. The definition of crazy is doing the same thing over, and over again, but expecting different results. Don't repeat your same debilitating patterns. Make conscious changes, and be aware of your thoughts and your emotions.

5

THE MILLIONAIRE MENTALITY

"Many people take no care of their money till they come nearly to the end of it, and others do just the same with their time." – Johann Wolfgang von Goethe

In a small town just east of Henryville, Indiana, in a small thin-walled shack, Wilbur and Margaret gave birth to a little baby boy named Harland. Harland was a gentle spirit and a kind soul, a boy who carried on the same traits as his father. But, a life of poverty weighed heavily on the small family. Making ends meet was a constant struggle for the Indiana parents of three. They toiled and worked for much of their lives, striving to get ahead, but there never seemed to be enough money to go around. It was a difficult time, and their struggles ran deep, affecting the children enormously.

To compound onto their struggles, Harland's father, who worked as a farmer, fell and broke his back when the young boy was just three years old. His father then spent the next two years struggling to work as a butcher in order to help keep up with the monthly expenses of the household. This was during the most influential years of Harland's youth, at a time when his personality was still taking shape and form. And, since times were so tough and money was so scarce, the children had to learn to get by on much less than most others. But, the tough times got even worse when Harland turned five, and fate struck his father down with a terrible fever, which he died from later that same day.

The sudden death of Harland's father was an enormous shock to the entire family. They were now faced with the dire situation of no income to support themselves with. Without a father to care for them, and provide financial support, they had to depend on their mother, who had never worked aside from running the household. Eventually, out of necessity, she found employment at a tomato-canning factory just to help make ends meet, but it was never enough. Harland was left having to help cook meals for the family, while his mother worked just to keep a roof over their heads.

At the age of 12, Harland's mother remarried, but his stepfather beat him. He suffered through emotional and physical tumult, and with his mother's blessing, he left the family home to move in with his uncle in the nearby town of Albany, Indiana. But, Harland wasn't happy there either. The emotional weight of his childhood was too much for him, and at the age of 15, after falsifying his date of birth, he enlisted in the army. He worked as a mule handler in Cuba during his service, but his enlistment only lasted for four months. After he received an honorable discharge, he went to live in Alabama with another uncle, where another of his brothers had also moved to escape his stepfather.

But, Alabama was no different for Harland. He held

many different odd jobs, and couldn't seem to hang onto any one in particular for too long. Nevertheless, in 1908, at the age of 28 years old, Harland married a woman by the name of Josephine, and they had three children together, two girls, and a boy. Things were looking up for Harland, but for one reason or another, he let life get the best of him again, and he was fired from yet another job due to insubordination. It was a low point in his life, and to make matters worse, his wife left him, and her brother wrote a letter to him calling him a "no-good fellow," who couldn't hold a job.

After everything that Harland went through in his life, after all the ups and the downs, in 1930 at the age of 40, he set out to open a service station in Corbin, Kentucky where he cooked chicken, steak, and country ham for customers from all over. He realized that the practice from his youth of cooking for his family had instilled some serious skills in him in the kitchen department. He was an excellent cook, and although he didn't have a restaurant, he served the food to customers next door, where he lived. Eventually, his popularity ballooned, and he moved his entire operation to a 142-seat restaurant in a nearby motel. It was there, over the next 9 years, that he developed his famous chicken recipe. It was there where he first learned to cook his chicken in a pressure cooker, as opposed to frying it, with his own blend of spices, for a quick and incredible meal. Word spread fast, and the critics raved about Harland's operation.

However, after all that work, Harland's restaurant failed in 1955, and at the age of 65 years old, he had virtually nothing left. After the failure of his restaurant, Harland decided to take his secret recipe for chicken, and a Social Security check in the amount of $105, and begin visiting restaurants to try to sell them on the idea of carrying his chicken. He donned his now-famous white suit, and set out on the road to try to convince anyone and everyone he could find to carry his chicken. He suffered 1,009 separate rejections from restaurants. One thousand and nine different people told him no, and told him that it would never succeed. Back then, the franchise model was a very new concept, and people weren't willing to try it.

However, Colonel Harland Sanders never gave up. He had the millionaire mentality. He knew that someone, somewhere, would eventually say yes to him. That first person came in the way of a restaurant located in Salt Lake City, Utah, over 1800 miles from his home in Kentucky. But, he knew that without a shadow of a doubt, even at the age of 65, after having faced so much failure in his life, he set out, made a goal, and succeeded. Today, Kentucky Fried Chicken restaurants are a global operation with over 18,000 franchises in 120 countries. Colonel Sanders succeeded in creating KFC into what it is today because he embodied the millionaire mentality. He dug deep down inside, and found that spirit within him that didn't let him give up. It told him that no matter how hard he needed to push, he was going to push that much harder. That's because if you want to make it in today's world, you have to push that hard.

THE POWER OF THE MIND

Our minds are very complex things, and even in today's day and age, scientists are yet to uncover all of the fascinating secrets of the mind. They haven't been able to unearth even a small fraction of the wonder of the mind, and all the things that it's capable of doing. Think about this for a moment, in your brain, you have billions upon billions of neurons – anywhere from 80 to 100 billion of them. Those neurons send signals to one another across gaps called synapses. Those signals do everything from allowing your body's organs to function autonomously, to springing any action forward that your mind wills your body to do. From walking, to sprinting, to solving complex problems, your mind does all of this. It does all of this with the aid of these neurotransmissions that are firing off in the mind. It's an incredible thing when you think about it. The complexities are simply marvelous. All of those things have come neatly together in one fine package to make you. You are the sum of all those tiny little parts – a genetically-engineered marvel.

When you stop to think about the complexities of life,

you can come to appreciate just how much is going on inside of you, without your being aware of it. From the blood that's pumping through your heart, to the 50,000 plus thoughts that are running through your mind on a daily basis, all of it happens without you having to do anything. You don't have to exert any effort just to make your lungs process the air, or for your kidneys to metabolize fat and insulin. None of it has to happen with your conscious thinking – it all happens behind the scenes. But, what's most important about this is, just how much your thoughts have an affect on your life. Those thoughts that are running through your mind are effecting your present situation and future outcomes, more so than you could ever even come to imagine. A simple thought can spring so much into action in your life. It can start and cause a chain of events that lead you towards your desired outcome.

Think about that for a moment. Think back to the past when you wanted something in your life, and you wanted it so badly. How did that thought-process begin? Where did it start? How did it spring into action and come into existence? What were the things that had to happen that led you from the simple thought, to bringing it into reality? How many numerous different events had to occur for that thought to become a reality? Of all the countless scenarios in life, somehow, you managed to make that thought come into being. You managed to will it into action. You manifested your dream into reality, no matter how big or small it was. Think about that for a moment. Maybe you envisioned a relationship in your past and it came to be, or maybe it was a car and it came to be. Or, maybe it was a trip somewhere in the world, and that came to be.

Thoughts are powerful. They are the epic vehicles that drive you towards your goals. And, those thoughts, when fueled by a sincere sense of action and effort, can lead you to accomplish anything, literally anything. No matter how many times you've heard this in the past, it's something that is worth repeating over, and over again – thoughts are things. The fact that so much can spring forward from a simple thought is incredible. We still haven't deciphered the mind, and all of its complexities that allow us to take a thought, and turn it into reality. The mind is so powerful that it can overcome any obstacle, and surmount any impediment. It doesn't matter what it is, if you can envision it, then you can achieve it or overcome it. Your mind is capable of doing that and so much more. We are only just scratching the surface with what we know about the mind and what it's capable of doing. All the things that the mind can accomplish to this day, constantly fascinates scientists from around the world.

Throughout the years, humankind has been able to accomplish so many things that they once considered being impossible. And, over the past 100 years, we've made more progress than we have in all of our existence. That says a lot for the potential of our race. It says a lot when a simple thought could spring forward with so much life, and come into reality to create something that was once only the subject of dreams. Could you imagine just fifty years ago being able to tell someone about the technology that exists today? Could you imagine being able to convey the speed and level of our communications, travel, and computing that exists at this very moment?

But, we all know about the pace and brevity of change and progress in our lives. We all know about the technological advances that we attribute to others in this world. We know that someone else was able to accomplish those things, that someone else was able to dream it up, and someone else was able to put thought into action. But, how about you? What do you have in your life today that was once just a thought? What exists today, right now, that you were once only able to just dream of? If you say nothing, then you aren't searching hard enough. Whether you've been through some tough times recently or not, you've been able to accomplish feats in the past that you once never thought you could do. Your thoughts became things.

Why is this important? The thought movement is critical to the millionaire method. It plays a major role in turning the invisible into the visible. It helps to take something that only exists in the mind, and turn it into reality. This thought movement is not something new; it's not a recent creation. Touted, discussed, hypothesized, and pondered on for centuries now, the thought movement has existed for quite some time. The power of the mind has impressed people throughout the ages, and they began to realize early on that thought could spring into reality. They began to harness the capability of the mind to build empires, conquer new lands, create new technologies, and overcome the seemingly impossible.

People throughout history have been able to achieve the seemingly impossible because they learned to harness their minds. They learned to dig deep down inside and pull through their difficult times because they conjured up the invisible. They were able to envision something that was bigger, brighter, and better for their lives, and they went out and accomplished it. But, nothing was achieved without action. They envisioned it in their minds, but they combined that special vision in their minds with action to create the magic recipe. Action fuels the invisible into the visible. Action brings forth things that used to be a dream, into reality.

When Colonel Harland Sanders, the creator of Kentucky Fried Chicken restaurants, went through one defeat and failure after another, he didn't give up. In his mind, he envisioned something better for his life. He knew, deep down inside, that he could achieve that vision.

He wasn't quite sure how it was going to happen. He didn't know the exact steps that were going to lead him there. No, he went out, every single day, and pushed at the age of 65. He pushed through any previous mental limitations that may have had held him back in the past. He pushed through until he had a breakthrough. His breakthrough took one thousand and nine different rejections. But, it only took one person to say yes to him. It only took one person to believe in his vision and his chicken recipe.

If Colonel Harland Sanders never mixed action with his vision, he would never have created his restaurants, which are now spread all over the world. Could you imagine if he had given up on the tenth rejection? Most people would have. Could you imagine if he had given up on the one-hundredth rejection? Or, even, just before he succeeded, could you imagine if he had given up on the one-thousandth rejection? He had the millionaire mentality. He could see his future. He knew what he was going to accomplish, and he knew it deep down inside. He had a vision, and it was a very powerful vision. It was so powerful in fact that once his vision took hold, it exploded across the world.

So, if you can imagine it, you can accomplish it. This is part of the millionaire mentality. But, it doesn't end with that. Yes, you must envision something, and fuel it with action, but there's more to the story. And, although that's an enormous part of the success recipe, there's more to it than just that. There's more than doing just that. The millionaire mentality involves a way of thinking. It moves from a state of debt and spending, to one of thrift, savings, and investment. Unfortunately, mainstream media helps to popularize the former. They love to chronicle the very wealthy as they travel the world and spend freely. But, the very wealthy are living off interest and passive income. They can afford to spend more freely. But, even in that instant, most of the average millionaires in the world implement the latter of savings and thrift. That's how they got rich in the first place. They didn't get rich by spending themselves into a hole, then working for a decade just to dig themselves out.

However, something that most people don't realize is that, some of the most successful people suffered through the biggest hardships. Did you know that Henry Ford went bankrupt at the age of 40? Of course, we all know that he went on to achieve eventual success, but he was met with huge hardships before that. And, Donald Trump went bankrupt at the age of 44, so did Walt Disney in 1921. There was also the bankruptcy of H.J. Heinz at the age of 31, Milton Hershey at the age of 23, Larry King at the age of 45, P.T. Barnum at the age of 46, and the list goes on. So many of these people suffered through many failures before succeeding, but they had the millionaire mentality. They knew, in their heart of hearts, that they would succeed. They had mentally envisioned it so vividly that they knew it was just a matter of time.

If you've failed, or you have a lot of debt, and you're wondering how you're going to succeed in life, remember all those that came before you. There were countless very successful men and women who failed so many times before they succeeded. You don't hear about much of that. You only hear about the successes of people, but you don't get to see what they went through, or where they came from. You don't get to see any of that information popularized unless you go digging for it. So, keep it in mind. As long as you have the millionaire mentality, and you take a clear, honest, and aware approach to your situation, envision your future, and fuel it with action, you will succeed. It won't happen overnight, but if you don't give up, you'll reach your goals. It just depends on how badly you want it.

Overall, though, the millionaire mentality is calculating. It's one where the numbers don't lie, and those same numbers go to good use in order to gauge and track the life of the millionaire. This is why it's so important to paint your financial picture. It's important to know where you stand in the world. It's important to be honest enough with yourself to look at the facts. Because, the longer you ignore the facts, the worse the financial picture will get. You have to rip off the scab, and force yourself to look. Force yourself to step away from your ego, and build awareness towards your present situation. Don't allow the ego to control you by keeping you in the dark. You will never get ahead in life if you do so.

Most of us know the story of John D. Rockefeller, the famous billionaire oil tycoon. But, did you know about his past? Did you know that, from an early age, his mother taught him to track all of his spending and income in a ledger? After his father disgraced the family through bigamy and philandering, John D. Rockefeller's mother instilled values of thrift and savings into him. But, even though his father ran off later in life, early on, he instilled certain values of commerce and trade that helped him grow his business into what it became. But, Rockefeller was smart enough to fuel his achievements through a vision for success, action, thrift, and savings. He reinvested his profits year after year, to constantly grow his enterprise by enormous proportions. He certainly had the millionaire mentality.

HAVING WHAT IT TAKES

It's easy to become frustrated with your present situation, and it's hard to see the forest through the trees at times. But, when you look at the bigger picture, and realize why you're doing what you're doing, you'll inch closer day after day to your goals. You'll make just a little bit of progress each time, and eventually move closer, until you succeed. In the beginning, when you're first starting out, things can seem frustrating. It can feel frustrating when it seems like all you're doing is trying to dig yourself out of a bad situation. But, you have to realize that it was by your own actions, and thoughts, that you ended up in that situation. It was because you continued to ignore what was in front of you, that things happened the way that they did.

No matter who you are or what you do, you've met some failures in life. We all have. We've all had those times when we just wanted to give up after failing again, and again. But, that's not having what it takes to succeed. That's not the millionaire mentality. Sure, all we hear about are the successes of the rich, but you must realize what it took to get them there. And, even when you talk about a very successful athlete who just seems gifted, you have to realize what it took to get that person to where he or she is today. The problem is that, most people don't see all that effort. They can't see all of the losses and the failures along the way. All they can see is the success portrayed to them. But, if you do the research, and see what that person went through to get to where they are, you'll come to appreciate the struggle.

The millionaire mentality really is a formula that takes an incredible amount of focus and willpower. You must be able to envision your success, and fuel it with action, be thrifty, save, and learn to invest your money. But, you must also have a strong will to succeed that won't allow you to give up. You see, willpower and perseverance are what push you through those present-day limitations. It's the perseverance and the will to succeed that will get you through the days when you just feel like quitting. But, when you quit, you lose the millionaire mentality. You can't quit, and you can't give up. You may fail time, and time again, but you can't give up. That's having what it takes.

But, we all know how hard it is when we encounter failure, to move past it. We all know how difficult it is to pick ourselves back up, and try again. We all know the pain and the emotions that are associated with failure. And, all too often, the ego makes it that much worse. The ego, which is protecting that fragile inner part of your inner self, can easily bruise. It can get bruised and very hurt, and then turn on you. It can help to create havoc in your life by launching you into a tirade of addictive behavior that only helps to mask the hurt and the pain it's trying to help you cover up. When this happens, you need to recognize it, and you need to correct it. You have to come to terms with the fact that failure is a part of life. If you've failed at something, it doesn't make you a lesser person. If you've failed over, and over, it doesn't mean that you don't deserve success.

All too often, failure acts as the final blow, making us crawl beneath our shells and seek the comfort of shelter, never to reemerge again. But, you can't allow life's failures to defeat you like this. You have to pull together the strength to continue on. Organize your mind, and your affairs, and push forward. Push forward even when everything inside of you is screaming for you to give up. That's how you make progress. That's how you achieve the seemingly impossible. It's okay to fail, and even if you've done it over, and over again, you're only human. But, in order to have what it takes, you must dust yourself off, and try again. You must do this, and continue to do it while organizing your mental faculties to support you. Don't engage in distractions that will only help to numb your emotions. Don't allow your bruised ego to launch you into a tirade of negative, or addictive behavior, only to mask the hidden truth in there. It's okay to feel hurt. It's okay to feel pain. It happens to everyone, but what doesn't happen to everyone is true success.

6

LEARNING TO PLAY BY THE RULES

"All the breaks you need in life wait within your imagination. Imagination is the workshop of your mind, capable of turning energy into accomplishment and wealth." – Napoleon Hill

Your ability to generate income is integral to the millionaire method, but so is learning to play by the rules. But, when I say learning to play by the rules, I'm talking about the millionaire method's rules. I'm talking about the rules that you must strictly adhere to, in order to get ahead, and stay ahead in life. I'm talking about the rules that separate the winners from the losers. All too often, life's pleasure-driven pursuits entangle us, only to later realize just how far behind we fell. We realize what our ill-gotten behavior, and habits have done to us. Then, we're in a panic to extricate ourselves from messy financial situations. Don't fall into these pitfalls. Don't allow life's very many distractions to tempt you, and lead you into an endless demise.

The reason why there's such a disparity in the world between the haves, and the have-nots, is that the former are able to strictly monitor their behavior, and temper their emotions. They're able to gather their entire mental, emotional, spiritual, and physical faculties, and point them in the right direction. They're able to micromanage the internal parts of their psychic apparatuses. They're so good at it in fact that they seemingly push further, and further ahead in life, with each passing day. As the successes build upon one another, they only compound, until they later explode in an unstoppable pattern of success. And, there's a lot to say about building this kind of momentum. There's a lot to say about allowing these small successes to compound on one another, day after day, to ultimately lead to huge successes in life.

But, we all know that's not the reality for most people. We all know that most people are living a life that's at the mercy of external influencers. They're not masters of their own domains, they're merely pawns in a global chess game; they're rats that are barely visible in the rat race. It's sad to see the world at such a grave state of affairs, but one can argue day and night as to the causes of what leads so many of the globe's population into these wealth traps. The signs are clear all around us, but people choose to ignore them. However, when you learn to play by the rules – as in, you follow the rules of the millionaire method – you know what to look out for in life. You know just what you should be doing, and what you shouldn't be doing. Although some of these rules can seem like common sense, they're broken all the time. They're broken in that pleasure-driven pursuit at the behest of the id.

Psychology plays such a major role in the millionaire method because it's at the very heart of our behavior; it's why we do the things that we do, why we make the choices that we make, and why we spend the way that we do. If you can understand the psychology of the millionaire mind, then you can make major strides towards implementing the ways of the millionaire method. But, as long as you allow your psychology to control your behavior, there's no way you can push ahead. There's no way to get ahead in a system that's designed to make you fall behind. For that reason, you have to play by the rules, and as hard as it may be to adhere to the rules, without doing so, you're really stifling your chances to succeed.

These rules go above and beyond creating that honest and open awareness to your current state of affairs. You have to do that first. You must first look at your situation with complete honesty, because otherwise, your ego still has a way to shroud its own behavior. The ego can continue to trick you into thinking there's more pain by confronting your present situation rather than not. The honesty in your financial picture is a prerequisite. You have to do those exercises, and you must be willing to pay attention to your thoughts by carefully analyzing your emotions. Once you've done those things, then, you have to learn to play by the rules.

WATCH YOUR SPENDING LIKE A HAWK

Whether you work for someone else or not, if you don't make more than you spend, you're violating one of the biggest principles of the millionaire method: *Rule #1: Always make more money than you spend.* But for most people, making more money than they spend is a stretch. They want to enjoy themselves. The pleasure pursuits of the id are overpowering in their psychic apparatuses. They just want to have a good time. They don't want to think about all the responsibilities that they have in the world. They want distractions, and they want emotion-numbing activities. Believe me, I know; I partook in this behavior for a very long time. But, it doesn't serve you. It only serves to help the ego numb everything else, and hide the truth from you. When you realize the truth, it's shocking and it's painful. The ego is trying to help you avoid that pain. It's doing everything in its power to keep it all a shrouded little secret.

If all of this sounds familiar to you, don't worry because you're not alone. You're not alone, because this is part of the built-in components of the psychic apparatus, developed, and derived, mainly through the psychosexual stages. That's why our psychology is so important to the millionaire method. Awareness is key. When you become aware of your own actions, and just how your psychic apparatus, and experiences, can work to limit you, you can take the steps to improve upon them. It doesn't mean that you have to feel bad for your present situation. There are far more people around the world in worse off situations than you. Be thankful for all that you have, but also work towards amending your situation. Take a little bit of action each and every day to set yourself back on the right track. Even if you've completely derailed, pick yourself back up again, and fix things.

Don't just sit there and allow life to constantly run you over. Become empowered, and envision success in your life. Envision it so vividly, that it almost becomes a reality in your mind. When you do this, you'll realize just how much more you can strive towards the fulfillment of your dreams, no matter what they are. If you can envision it, and build it, you will succeed. Steadily build upon your successes day after day, working slowly towards the attainment of your dreams. But, you have to really do the work. If you see that you're spending more money than you make each month, this is the first cardinal rule of the millionaire method that you're breaking. And, as hard as it may be for you to spend less than you earn, you must adjust your financial life in order to get ahead. If you continue on the same track of accumulating debt, and spending money frivolously, you'll end up in a far worse situation, month after month.

To stick by this rule, make sure you created a financial budget. Ensure that you know just how much money you have left over each month. Don't go poking around in the dark. If you didn't do the exercises, go back and do them now because they're critical for your success. When you paint that financial picture and set a monthly budget for yourself, you can meticulously track and analyze your progress. Don't guestimate any of it. Force yourself to look at your bills, and calculate things each month. If you continue to ignore them, and go on living the same way, you can't expect different results. Make a promise to yourself to live differently. Make a promise to yourself to make the sacrifices that are required to make to truly get ahead.

Just think about how much there is to look forward to when you can live by this rule. Imagine how good it will feel to actually have money left over each month that doesn't go out the door frivolously. It will feel good, and it will get your mind searching for ways it can grow that money. After several months of being meticulous with your spending, you'll look for ways you can invest that money; it will become natural to you. But, you can't allow yourself to slip into spending that extra money, because that's not the purpose of the exercise. You have to watch your spending like a hawk. This is critical for the millionaire method.

SAVING MONEY

By making more money than you spend, it allows you to set aside funds for savings. If you're not saving every single month, then you're not implementing the millionaire method, because that is the second rule to the millionaire method: *Rule #2: Save at least 10% of your income every month.* When you make it a habit to save a portion of your income, it does a couple of things. Firstly, it sends a signal to your brain of abundance. When you can tell your mind that there is more than enough, your mind has a very powerful way of seeing things differently.

In a state of abundance, the mind operates much differently than when it's in a state of lack. When it's in a state of lack, the internal tensions and conflicts in your mind begin to place a great deal of pressure on your physiology, and your body suffers. You see signs of stress materialize through things like lack of sleep, high blood pressure, abnormal eating, heart problems, digestive problems, and so on. When the body is in this state of lack, the senses heighten, and the anxiety and fear levels in your body increase. Anything small can set this person off.

If you've been in a state of lack before, you know how it feels to have the walls closing in on you. You know how small you feel in comparison to the world. When this happens, the ego searches for a way out. It searches for ways to dull the pain, instead of dealing with it head on.

However, living in a state of abundance is much different. When you pay yourself first, and in effect save at least 10% of your income on a monthly basis, something shifts in your mind. A powerful internal shift moves you from being mentally inferior, to becoming empowered. A strong mental shift occurs, which can help to fuel you towards your goals. Because, when you don't live in abundance, and you can't save at least 10% of your income, you are walking a fine line of financial catastrophe. Save at least 10% of your income, if not more. If you can afford to save more, do so immediately.

And if you say that you physically can't save any money each month, then that's when you truly must save money each month. No matter what your financial obligations are, you have to pay yourself first. You have to pay yourself first no matter what. When you do this, your mind will find ways to pay everything else off by cutting corners where it's necessary. There are always ways to cut out extraneous spending each month. No matter what you do, or who you are, you can always save money. Regardless of it all, you must find a way to pay yourself first. You must do this if you want to implement the millionaire method.

When the mind lives in this state of abundance, not only does it feel like it's making progress, but your mind will automatically begin to explore the possibilities of putting that money to good use. You cannot allow yourself to fall back into the habits of more spending, and creating more debt. You cannot allow yourself to go backwards, especially when you work hard to save that money. No matter what happens, you must keep the money that you save in savings, or put it towards investments. This is not your emergency fund, or your shopping fund; and it's not a fund that you can dip into to take a vacation. You see, this is where most people go wrong; this is where most people entangle themselves. When they see money burning a hole in their pockets, they look for ways to spend it. Don't fall into this trap, because it's one of the biggest wealth traps in the world today. Don't ever spend money set aside for savings. Ever.

It's not only about saving the money and keeping it there; it's about investing it. Not only that, if you spend that money, for example to place on the down payment of a new car lease, the real cost of spending that money, far exceeds the value of the money in the first place. Far too many people are attracted to the low monthly payments that exist. It makes it far too easy to accumulate more, and more debt. It makes it simple to just charge it, or worry about paying it off later. This happens when the anticipatory effect of the purchase, exceeds the logical, and cognitive realizations of its real cost to you. The mind doesn't calculate just how much money you'll be paying in interest for that shiny new object. All it sees is the shiny new object, and the pleasure-driven id does all that it can to convince your ego to just say yes.

Have you ever found yourself in this situation? Have you ever gotten ahead, only to later find yourself falling behind because you didn't stick to your guns? This happens to everyone, and if you've been in this trap, you know how very tempting it can be. But, when you fall into this wealth trap, you set yourself back immensely. Not only do you have your existing debt to worry about, but also by accumulating more of it, you are essentially defeating your chances of getting ahead in life. You're killing off any opportunities you may have to invest that hard-earned money you placed in savings.

THE ROOF OVER YOUR HEAD

The next rule in the millionaire method is: *Rule #3: Own the Roof over your Head.* No matter what, you must make it a priority to own the roof over your head. Over the years, real estate has been the number one most beneficial investment that families have made over time. When you don't own the roof over your head, you're helping someone else pay their mortgage. But, not only are you doing that, you're also taking away from your own potential investment by lining someone else's pockets. Every month that money goes towards rent, rather than towards your own mortgage, is a month further away from creating real and lasting wealth.

If you say that you can't afford a house or an apartment to live in, then you're not digging deep enough. You may enjoy renting because it affords you the luxury of having a nicer place for less money, but all that does is to serve the ego. You have to dig deep if you want to succeed in life. You have to make some serious sacrifices. In addition, the tax benefits of owning a home are extraordinary. And since you're going to be paying a lot of taxes in this life, especially as your income increases, positioning yourself for tax savvy investments, even as basic as owning your own home, is paramount.

No matter what you have to do, and no matter whom you have to speak to, you have to make it a goal to own the roof over your head. If you're too scared to find out if you quality for a mortgage, try it anyways. Go and speak to a professional that can help. No matter how basic the living standards may be, owning will always outweigh the benefits of renting. And if you can't qualify, no matter what you do, then find out what you need to do in order to qualify for a home loan. Then, make that your goal, and work towards it. This way, you have a target you can focus all of your energy on. You can move towards something aside from just blindly saving and investing for the future, because a home to call your own is your future. Always make this a priority, no matter what.

There's also a certain sense of pride that comes along with owning your own home. There's a certain sense of pride in that ownership that you simply don't get when you're renting. When you're renting, you can't make any improvements to the property, and if you do, that money is going to waste. You would only be paying to improve someone else's property, and increase their bottom line. You don't get that same sense of satisfaction of walking through the doors of your own home when you're renting. You realize each time that you're only helping someone else get richer. You're only helping someone else to increase the property owner's bottom line.

Make it a priority, right now, if you don't own your own home, to schedule an appointment with a mortgage broker. Go online, right this instant, find a broker near you, or several brokers, and call them. Actually call them and make an appointment, then go and sit down with them. Something visceral occurs when you sit down with a mortgage broker face to face. The dream of owning a home becomes all that much more real. It doesn't happen just by sending in email inquiries. It doesn't happen unless you make it feel more real. Furthermore, sitting down in person helps to materialize that thought into action. Something that once only existed in your mind, is suddenly much more real, because you're taking action and speaking to a professional who can help to make that dream a reality.

However, all too often, people are mentally stifled with the fear of speaking to someone else about their financial situation. They're too afraid to explain their situation to someone else because they can't bear to know the truth themselves. They don't want to look at their own financial picture, let alone have someone else look at their financial picture. This fear can be so great that it holds you back from progressing. This fear can be so immense that it zaps the life right out of you. The only fear that exists is in your mind. You can overcome that fear with action. What's the worst that can happen? You can be rejected, so what? Rejection and failure are part of life. Do you remember how Colonel Sanders went to one thousand and nine chicken restaurants before someone said yes to him? Well, thirty-one publishers rejected Stephen King's first novel. Thirty-one. And, twelve separate publishers rejected J.K. Rowling's Harry Potter. Twelve! Can you imagine how they felt after they saw the enormity of their successes? But, they didn't give up. They never stopped believing in themselves.

Could you imagine if those people stopped before they succeeded? Do you think that getting a home mortgage is any different from that? Of course it's not. If you're committed to the goal of owning your own home, you'll find a way. The mind has a way of blazing a trail, even in the midst of adversity. When Thomas Edison set out to invent the light bulb he failed over ten thousand times.

But, he didn't give up; he kept pushing until he found a way to make it work.

When you put your mind to something, all the obstacles topple over like dominoes. It will start slow at first, and then progress rapidly, but you must not give up. Once you give up, the chain will break, and the dominos will stop falling. The obstacles won't go away if you give up, and in fact, they will be harder to overcome if you quit trying. You must keep persevering, again, and again, no matter how many times it takes. That's how you achieve true success. That's the millionaire method.

MIND YOUR BUSINESS

Rule #4: Mind your own Business. In today's world, it's extremely difficult to get ahead if you don't mind your own business. What does this mean? Well, if you don't already own your business, then it's imperative that you do so. Owning your own business is integral to the millionaire method. Even if you work for someone else, and can't afford to quit your full time job right now, start a business on the side. It will take you time to successfully launch and promote your business anyhow, and you can do this in your spare time to start.

No matter who you are, or where you live in the world, you can start your own business. In fact, starting your own business is the quickest pathway to riches, but you must follow all the other rules of the millionaire method. You must also paint your financial picture, and approach your current state of affairs in an honest and forthright manner. And although successfully getting a business off the ground will take time, it's what you need to do in order to achieve any notable success. This is not to say that working for someone else won't allow you to live a comfortable lifestyle. Sure, you can live comfortably, but you won't achieve true financial freedom unless you mind your own business.

If you're scared of owning your own business, or unsure of what type of product or service you would provide, it's a fear you must get over. Owning your own business takes a lot of work, yes, that's very true, but it's also one of the most rewarding things you can do in life. Not only do you get to be your own boss, but also you get to call the shots. You get to say when you start the day, and when you end it. You get to choose the things that you do with your time to best serve your business. Yes, owning a business takes discipline, but the millionaire method is all about discipline. You cannot expect to get far ahead in life by working a nine-to-five and helping someone else build their business. It's similar to not owning your own home. When you don't own your own business, you're merely making the business owner rich, not yourself.

If you're unsure of what product or service you would provide, you must dig deep. There are many different online sources for providing a product or service. You must first choose a business type, and then select what you'll be providing. With a minimal amount of research and investment, you can quickly start up your own company and be in business for yourself, no matter where you live. No matter what it is you want to do – whatever goods or services you want to provide – you can do it. The best part is that if you work a full time job, you can use your spare time to build that business. Don't have spare time? Cut out all the other time wasters that you currently engage in. Stop surfing the Web so much, stop browsing through social media, stop playing games on your phone, or stop watching television. There is time in the day, always, just like there's always ways to cut your spending and expenses. If you search hard enough, you'll find the time; if you search long enough, you can figure out a way. There's always a way.

The most successful people in the world have started businesses and they've failed numerous times over. But it was through those failures that they finally learned the secrets to success. It was through the constant trial-and-error that they were able to unlock the ways in which they should operate. But, the ones who achieved true success did it by applying the millionaire method. You must operate your life as if it was a business, and you must operate a business and mind it like a hawk. Don't pay attention to the naysayers. Don't allow the negativity from others to suck you down and allow you to doubt yourself. Never doubt yourself, because you can do anything you put your mind to; literally anything. Imagine what's been accomplished in this world when people put their minds to it. The evidence is all around you. What once was a dream in the heart of one person became a reality. That computer in your house, that phone in your pocket, and that car that you drive – they were all once something in one person's mind. It was a thought from the invisible that came into the visible.

DEATH AND TAXES

Rule #5: Tax Planning. Benjamin Franklin is famous for coining the phrase, "In this world nothing can be said to be certain except death and taxes." The millionaire method requires a strict adherence to tax law. If you plan to accumulate wealth, you must be mindful of taxes. You must understand tax laws and plan your finances accordingly, to achieve the greatest benefit in tax deductions possible. Now, you should certainly consult with an accountant or a tax attorney when doing anything, because each individual person has his or her own unique situation.

But, what it really comes down to is planning. You must plan your tax situation, and understand how taxes work in your own city, state, and country. You must understand intrinsically how and where your tax dollars go, and how you can setup the most optimal tax situation for yourself. To do this, you have to consult with an accountant or a tax attorney in your area. The small amount of money invested in the beginning of your endeavors, can save you a whole lot of money and grief later down the road. Be sure to plan accordingly once you understand your tax situation and how to create the most optimal taxation setup for your business and personal life.

If you work for an employer now, you might think about taxes less than you would if you're working for yourself. If you're self-employed, or plan on opening up a new business, then you need to worry about taxes. You need to understand just how taxes work in your area. The problem is that, many people don't plan for taxes, and they end up getting burned, especially when their pleasure-driven id is pushing them to spend money when they can't afford to do so. Later down the road, it comes back to haunt you when the tax man cometh. Be careful, plan, and act accordingly. Don't fall into the wealth trap of overspending, then not having enough to pay your taxes.

ADD VALUE TO THE WORLD

The last rule of the millionaire method is – *Rule #6: Always Add Value to the World.* If you want to get rich doing something in this world, an important rule you must keep in mind is that you must always be adding value to the world. No matter what you're engaged in – whatever task is at hand – be it for your employer, or for a customer of your own business, you must always add value. You always have to provide more value in exchange for the money that you're taking. Whether you're selling goods, or services, they must be of more value than the cost that you're selling them for. And, if you work for an employer, you must always give that employer 110% of your effort, and provide more value to the employer than he or she is paying you in wages.

Why do you need to add value? Well, what most people don't realize is that, doing the bear minimum to get you by, will never get you ahead. Sure, it may make your ego feel empowered for getting the best of a deal somewhere, but it won't serve you in the long term. When you don't provide more value to someone than the goods, services, or time that you're exchanging it for, people take notice. They take notice, and after some time passes they realize that they can do without those goods, services, or time that you're offering. That's because there's a hundred different replacements for what you're providing, so don't give anyone an excuse to look elsewhere. And, when you provide an exceedingly high value in exchange for your goods, services, or time, then that's when you can truly excel in this world. It's all about providing value, no matter what you do. Always pay attention to the details, and ensure you're providing value. Always.

I don't think that I can stress this point enough. If you set out to do something, no matter how menial that job may seem to you at the time, set out to do it at the best of your capabilities. It doesn't matter it what it is, how small, or how large, you must do it to the best of your abilities. Even if you think that doing less work is okay to get you by, you should go above and beyond the call of duty, always. When you do this, people will take notice and pay attention. This is how word of mouth travels, and good reputations are born, and fostered. This is also the way to increasing things like market share, because when you provide great value, word travels fast. But, if you provide poor value, word will travel even faster. Don't make the mistake in life of not providing a great deal of value. Always keep that in the back of your mind.

7

THE FIVE CRUCIAL MILLIONAIRE TRAITS

"In order to succeed, your desire for success should be greater than your fear of failure." — Bill Cosby

Millionaires around the world have much more in common than just wealth, and financial freedom. They all possess a certain set of traits that act as a prerequisite to achieving that financial freedom. By possessing these traits, or aspiring to possess them, you can embody the millionaire mentality, and properly implement the millionaire method. Ever since the dawn of economies, humankind has strived to succeed in life. No matter where they were, or who they were, they aspired to achieve the goal of financial freedom. But, what does that take? Aside from our discussions up until this point, to become a millionaire you must harbor these five traits. You must embody them whole-heartedly, and viciously exhibit them.

The millionaire method isn't just about learning to play by the rules. The rules are critical to the millionaire method, but you must also embody the millionaire traits as well. You must be able to inherently harbor these traits in order to excel in the macro-game of life. The rules focus on the micro, as those rules apply to your financial spending patterns. They involve your personal financial decisions to do things like save money, watch your spending, mind your business, add value, and understand taxes. However, they don't encompass the traits that you must possess as you go about implementing the rules. The traits are what help you amongst society and economy to excel in the game of life. They are what help others to look at you with a sign of respect, and admiration for being the master of your own domain. But, that personal domain, also reflects through the macro-domain. Your personal domain has to interact with others' personal domains, so it's highly critical that you master it. It's highly critical that you ensure you're embodying the traits to push you ahead and keep you there.

After you read the traits, and absorb them, you'll have more of an appreciation of just what people have to go through in order to achieve success. Unfortunately, they don't give us these tools through formal education. They don't teach us how to succeed in life. They only tell us to work hard, go to school, and get a good job. That doesn't cover everything else in between. Without the proper financial education, most people wallow away in misery, and despair. But, had they learned the rules, traits, and painted their financial pictures in an honest way, they could have understood just what it takes to succeed.

Success is hard. No one can ever promise you that success is going to be easy. As soon as you see someone claiming their product or service is going to easily, and quickly make you rich, run the other direction as fast as you can. You have to be much more realistic about true and lasting wealth accumulation. You have to look at it with a wide-eyed determination that's not going to fade as the years go by. For some, not having this instant gratification answer to success can be frustrating. It can be frustrating when they realize the severity of the task. The millionaire method is hard to achieve, and it takes work. It takes a sincere amount of effort, and determination, to realize your dreams.

These traits embody the successful millionaires today. They encompass so much of what's required and demanded of a person with any power and authority today. When you don't embody these traits, you may see success, but it will be fleeting. It won't last long. Success can never last for very much time if you can't embody these traits. Make sure that whatever you do, from this day forward, you do it with these five traits in mind. You will find yourself having difficulty with it at first, but as time goes by, you'll realize how integral these traits are to succeeding to any noticeable degree.

TRAIT #1 – HONESTY & INTEGRITY

The most important trait central to the millionaire method is honesty and integrity. Throughout the world, men and women have vied to achieve great success, but have failed for a variety of reasons. One of the biggest reasons for failure has been lack of honesty and integrity. No matter what you do for a living, you must always be honest in all your dealings. Your word must be your bond, no matter what. If you make a promise to someone, you must live up to it. You must do anything and everything to honor your promises, and your word. From paying your bills on time, to fulfilling a promise in business to deliver certain goods or services at a pre-agreed-upon price, and at a pre-agreed-upon time, you must always be honest and harbor a great deal of integrity in all your dealings.

When you're not honest, and you don't honor your word and your commitment, news spreads fast. It spreads much faster than had you honored it. That's because bad news travels very fast. Think about it. In today's society, communication is at light speed, and when someone does something wrong, people enjoy putting that person on blast. If you don't want to have your name tarnished, you must be honest and forthright. You must honor your word; if you said you'd do something, you better do it, or risk suffering the consequences.

In addition, when you're honest and forthright, people will begin to trust you. They will trust you with many things, and entrust their business to you. You must not break their trust. You must never break their trust no matter what. If you do, you can risk losing it all. You can forget about becoming a millionaire, because you'll have difficulty barely getting by. No matter what, honest and integrity is paramount to the millionaire method. It's easy to talk about all the things you can do to increase your net worth, but as soon as you start dishonoring your commitments, and breaking your word, it can all go downhill fast. Just think about some of the examples of celebrities and notable businesspersons who have suffered through this. News of their shortcomings and their indiscretions travels fast. Whether or not mainstream media exploits them is irrelevant, because had they been honest and had integrity in the first place, they would have remained exalted. Instead, they suffered the consequences and severe embarrassment.

Never allow yourself to slip into this type of a situation. Never tarnish your name through careless mistakes. And, if you make mistakes, own up to them. Don't lie about them. Admit them, and make them right. Do everything in your power to make them right. It doesn't matter what you did, because people make mistakes, as long as you right the wrongs, people can learn to forgive. And, although it's better not to make the mistakes in the first place, we're all human. Don't let the pleasure-driven pursuits of the id put you in a bad spot. Don't allow the id to push you to spend money that you can't afford to spend. When you back yourself up against the wall, you will be harming yourself and others that trust in you. Don't ever abuse that trust.

Never.

TRAIT #2 – SKILLS MASTERY

In a book called *Outliers*, Malcolm Gladwell claims that to master any skill, a person is required to put in 10,000 hours of practice or effort. No matter what the skill is, the argument is that, to master it requires 10,000-hours. And, in order to achieve the millionaire method, you must master your skill, whatever that may be. You must harbor the trait of skill mastery. Whatever it is that you decide to do in the world – whatever goods or services you plan on selling – you must master your area of expertise. Whatever that area is, you must master it. In the beginning, learning a new skill is difficult. Whether you take up Website design, software development, jewelry craftsmanship, stock trading, or anything else, you must master that skill.

The difficulty is that mastery is hard. Mastery of a skill takes an enormous amount of effort and exertion. It also takes a tremendous amount of failures before truly getting something right. It takes multiple setbacks before you can truly achieve mastery level. The only difference between someone who becomes a master in a skill, and someone who doesn't, is perseverance. To become a master, you can't give up. Even when the going gets tough, you can't throw the towel in. You must learn to push on, even in the face of great failure or adversity. But, once you've mastered your skill, the tasks become easier. It becomes much easier to institute and implement your chosen area of labor once you've mastered the skill at hand. It becomes effortless. But, until then, you must work tirelessly to master that skill, and it will pay off in spades.

This is integral to the millionaire method, because the reason why so few people succeed at life and in business is that they give up. They give up before they're even close to mastering a skill. They give up because their egos bruise, egos that work to tell them that they don't need to continue that pursuit. It tells them that it's okay to throw in the towel, and that they never really wanted it that badly anyways. But, as time goes by, and a person looks back, they begin to regret not having continued that pursuit. They realize that, had they not given up, life would have been much different for them. They realize that, had they persevered and mastered their skill, things would have been enormously different.

Don't allow yourself to give up. Don't allow yourself to throw in the towel just like that. Learn to master a skill, and when you commit to doing something, make sure you follow through. Put all of your energy into mastering a skill, and becoming the best that you possibly can be at it. Set the bar high, and inch towards that every day. Make sure you give it all you have; even when you feel like you can't give it any more, keep pushing. Keep pushing, and pushing, until you can't push any more, then push just a little bit more. Eventually, you will succeed. Eventually, you'll master that skill. But, until then, remember it's going to be hard. No matter what skill you decide to focus on, it's going to be extremely hard to become a master at it. But, time's going to pass by quickly, and with each passing day, you'll become better, and better. This is paramount to the millionaire method.

TRAIT #3 – COMMUNICATION

To embody the millionaire method, you must become an expert communicator. You must learn to communicate your thoughts, regardless of the situation. Whether you're communicating with your debt collectors, while selling your goods or services, with business investors, or anyone else, you must be an excellent communicator. This is part of the millionaire method because, without communication skills, one can't possibly expect to succeed with any great degree. Since communication lies at the heart of all that we do, it also lies at the heart of the millionaire method. People expect to encounter a great communicator when dealing in the professional world.

Just think about it yourself. Think about all the times when you've tried to communicate with people, but grew frustrated. An inability to communicate puts people off, no matter what the situation. Whether it's in business or in your personal life, if you can't properly express your emotions, and communicate your intellect, you can't expect to succeed. You can't expect to embody the millionaire method and assimilate a millionaire mentality without excellent communication skills. And throughout history, the world's millionaires and billionaires have always been excellent communicators. From politicians, to highly esteemed businesspersons, those who can communicate the most effectively are always the ones on top.

But, communication skills don't come easy, especially when the ego has its way. When the ego interferes, communication becomes exponentially difficult. That's because the ego wants to have its cake and eat it too. It doesn't want to ever feel like it's wrong or fallible; it doesn't want to communicate, it just wants to be right. If you can't communicate from an honest and intelligent perspective, you can kiss all chances of success goodbye. Whether you have to practice communication until you're blue in the face, speak to a therapist, or take communication courses, you must master the art of communication. Learn the skill of communicating effectively, and do it with tact.

Just think about your communication skills for a moment. Just think about how important it is to effectively communicate, no matter what capacity of life you engage in. If you shy away from communication, or you exhibit passive-aggressive behavior that limits your communication skills, it should be your top priority to fix this. You must create awareness and come to the realization that communication is integral to your success in life. Most successful people are leaders, and all leaders are excellent communicators. If you can't communicate, you will severely limit your millionaire potential, and you certainly won't embody the millionaire method.

TRAIT #4 – CONVICTION

The fourth trait of the millionaire method is conviction. When you have conviction in something, you're devoted, and you'll do whatever it takes to succeed at it in life. With true conviction, you can conquer any goal, and surmount any obstacle. Nothing can stand in your way. Conviction is also part of what allows you to persevere when you hit severe amounts of adversity, or you experience a great deal of struggle while attempting to reach your goals.

In business, and in life, you must be able to make quick decisions, and stick to them. You must be able to stay convicted, and committed. That is the hallmark of the millionaire method. That is what it takes to achieve great success in life. Because, when you make slow decisions, and you change them quickly, you're bound to run into one wall after another. However, when you can quickly decide on what you want, then push towards it with conviction and not give up, eventually you will reach your goal. Eventually, you will overcome your obstacle. But, all too often today, people don't stay convicted. They don't stay committed to what they set out to achieve. They quickly give up. If you find yourself falling into this wealth trap, recognize it quickly, because the ego will do what it takes to shroud this. It will work against you to cover up this shortcoming.

As we've seen, the ego does a lot to limit us in our pursuits of our dreams. It does it because it doesn't want to suffer through the pain and the hard work. It wants to achieve things easily. It wants you to simply kick your feet back up and relax. It doesn't want you to have to work hard, tirelessly without end, to achieve your goals. It doesn't want you to have to fight the demons inside your mind that are just telling you to indulge in those pleasure-driven pursuits. The id is all-powerful in the mind. The id can do a lot to limit your quest in the millionaire method. It will do all that it can to force you into those emotion-numbing activities. It will tell you to smoke one more cigarette, when you're trying to quit. It will tell you to eat one more candy bar, when you're trying to lose weight. And it will tell you it's okay to spend just one more time, when you're trying to save.

It's no wonder there's such a disparity between the rich and the poor. It's no wonder that there's such a difference between the haves and have-nots. The gap keeps widening because the fact of the matter is, that it's difficult to conquer those demons. It's difficult to keep the id in check. As you've come to see, so much of our psychology, stemming from before we can even recollect, has limited us. So much of our personality has taken footing so early on, that it's virtually impossible to be able to overcome it without an honest awareness towards it. It's impossible to look at yourself and see that what you're doing is wrong, especially when you don't have the knowledge and the expertise to know what you're looking for. That's due to the design of the ego, which helps to shroud that. It doesn't want you to see that. It doesn't want you to realize what it's trying to do. It doesn't want you to work your tail off to embody the millionaire method. It wants things to come easy. But we all know that things don't come easy, and they never will.

This is also why so many people get sucked into the get-rich-quick schemes, and the fast-weight-loss diets. It's because people want the instant gratification of what these systems are offering. They don't want to work hard at it; they just want it to be given to them. This is not entirely because people are lazy, it's because the design of the ego dictates us to do this. It dictates us to do this because it's trying to satisfy the pleasure-driven id within reality. If a program sounds good, and looks good, then it must be good. But, what people come to find is that, these systems take a lot of work, and as soon as people realize this, they tend to quit. When they don't have conviction in their hearts, they'll quit anything. Don't fall into this trap. Have conviction in your life no matter what it is you're striving towards. Eventually, you'll reach your goal, but it won't happen overnight.

TRAIT #5 – ADAPTABILITY

The millionaire method requires you to be many things, but it also requires you to be able to adapt to things. You must be able to adapt to the changing environment, whether that be in your business, or in your personal life, because if you can't adapt, you can't survive. And, if you can't survive, you certainly won't thrive, and the millionaire method is all about thriving. No matter what happens in your life – what changes you may encounter – you have to be able to adapt yourself to those changes. One of the biggest things that really kill millionaires-in-the-making is the inadaptability to adapt. People are such creatures of habit that they're unable to change their focus enough to see all the change that's occurring around them.

This is as big for people as it is for companies. Just think about all of the companies that have been unable to adapt to a changing business environment, and have subsequently gone bankrupt. It happens all the time, and mainstream media loves to glorify these situations. It loves to see people and businesses get cut back down to earth. But it also calls forward the importance of adapting. Our genetics is the sum of adaptation over millions of years; it's in your genes to be able to adapt. However, some people remain too stubborn to adapt, and the changing tides of life clobber them.

You must do your best to adapt to whatever is going on in your life. For example, if you lose your job, or you lose a customer base, you must make changes to your financial spending, and reorganize your life, or suffer a slow and painful financial death. You have to be able to see what's happening around you, and not turn a blind-eye to it. The problem is that, with the ego and id in the way, it's very easy to allow your pride and your pleasure-driven pursuits to get the best of you. You have to ensure that you can adapt to the situation, whatever that situation may be. And, if you go into business for yourself, watch it carefully, be meticulous in your analysis of all things, and it will pay off enormously down the road.

8

THE PASSIVE INCOME GAME

"When your outgo exceeds your income, the upshot may be your downfall." – Paul Harvey

In today's world, most people succumb to a nine-to-five job. They really have no other option. In order to support themselves in society, they have to seek an active income. They have to seek a way that they can actively work each day in order to generate a stream of income. Most people have to go out there into the cruel world, wake up each day, and work. Sometimes, that work is hard labor, forcing folks to exert a tremendous amount of energy just to produce a daily income. Other times, the work is mental labor, forcing the taxing of peoples' minds that naturally occurs under tremendous amounts of the stress, and pressures of a job that doesn't cease to relent with its obligations. Most people – especially those who are salaried – are married to their jobs. They literally have to work around the clock just to keep up with the demands of the workload.

What's worse is that, for those people who are working those very mentally and physically taxing jobs, that also have a very heavy debt load to carry, the stress levels seem to compound upon one another. They have to work tirelessly, in a very demanding job, just to support their debt and spending. Then, in order to release that built up energy and stress, they delve into more pleasure-driven pursuits, thus pushing them further and further behind. This vicious cycle has been designed to help line the pockets of the pleasure-driven corporations, ready and willing to sell you anything from alcohol, to tobacco, to sex, to entertainment, and everything in between. They are willingly waiting with their credit card machines and cash registers to accept your money, as they catch you in the wealth traps.

All of this may sound a little bit dramatic, but it's entirely true. The inherent design of the system sets the average person back. The inherent design of the system wrings as much money out of a person through revolving debt, expenses, and interest payments, as humanly possible. They want you to lease that new car, buy that overpriced home, and stock-up on all the liquor and beer you can afford. They know just how to lure the people in, they've been doing it for decades now, and they will continue to do it. If you can't break yourself out of the system that's designed to hold you back, then getting ahead is virtually impossible.

However, getting ahead isn't impossible. If you can play by the rules and embody the millionaire traits, you can get ahead, but it's not going to happen overnight. Over time, however, it will happen. It will happen slowly, it will compound upon itself, and little by little, you will start to get ahead. And, slow and steady wins the race in this case. Sure, many people get sucked into the late-night infomercials touting the next get-rich-quick scheme, but just like anything else, those systems take work. The reason why so many people fail at those is they simply give up. They give up on whatever it is that they decided to pursue in the first place because they didn't see instant results. When people don't see instant results, they're very quick to throw in the towel. They're quick to make the decision that they don't want to pursue that hope or that dream anymore.

The truth of the matter is that diving into the passive income game is hard work. No matter what anyone tells you, it's going to take you countless hours of time investment on the front-end, to make money on the back-end. This hard and grueling work isn't for everyone, but it is for the people that want to employ the millionaire method, because there's just nothing like passive income. You can do all the active income work you want, but there's just something so much more satisfying about passive income. There's something so very satisfying about the fact that you can continue to collect money on end, for something that you no longer have to put any work into. Granted, there's a lot of effort involved in the front-end, but it's worth it. It's worth it because you get to see that effort really pay you back in spades. It continues on and on, long after you've forgotten about the work done in the first place.

GENERATING PASSIVE INCOME

Over the years, I've read hundreds of self-development books. I've covered just about every topic you can possibly imagine. But the one thing that always irked me about the ones that were dedicated to financial success, were they left me feeling high and dry. I wanted to find real methods that could make me money, and not just read about all the theory behind it. But, that's where I used to go wrong. Years and years ago, I thought the answer was simple for me – I needed to find a way to produce huge amounts of income. But what happened was, no matter how much money I was able to make, I seemed to spend just as much in those pleasure-driven pursuits. The answer wasn't necessarily in generating more income; it was in understanding the principles behind keeping, and re-investing the income, you generated.

I came to the realization that no matter how hard I worked, that I would never be able to get ahead if I didn't deal with what was at the heart of the matter. If I didn't embody the millionaire traits, and play by the rules of the millionaire method, I would never truly get ahead. Even after making more money in one year than most people see in a lifetime, I kept falling behind. That realization for me came a very long time ago, but it was a very slow and painful realization. It was a way of thinking and behaving that took the focus of every mental, emotional, spiritual, and physical faculty for me to overcome. That's because the id was so powerful in me. I focused so hard on those pleasure-driven pursuits, that everything else blinded me. The ego didn't want me to see the truth. If I had seen the truth, it would have meant a lot of pain. And the pain certainly did come when I finally did see the truth, a lot of pain.

But, it doesn't have to be that way for you. It doesn't have to be a very painful process. And although it takes a lot of work, you can slowly dig yourself out of whatever hole you've dug for yourself. You can slowly come out on top, but you can't expect it to happen overnight. The problem is that, with so many obligations, people find it hard to find the time to focus. But that's only because they refuse to give up their pleasure-driven pursuits. They refuse to stay at home and plan, when all they want to do is go out and be with friends. They refuse to buckle down and take a hard, and honest look at their situation, when all they want to do is have fun.

Although there may be many things holding you back, including yourself, you must look at the situation from an angle that will help you to get ahead. It's clear that, for most people at least, their incomes from their active employment just doesn't cut it. There never seems to be enough. There's always the need for more. You have to first tackle this root of your behavioral problems when it comes to money, before moving on. But, the question remains, how do you generate more income? How do you find more ways that you can make money without having to work so hard? Passive income streams, that's how. Although passive income isn't the sole answer to the quest for wealth, it's certainly a major component of it. If you can successfully tackle your present situation, first by eliminating debt, reducing your spending, increasing your saving, and investing your money, then you're ready for passive income streams.

WHAT IS PASSIVE INCOME?

Passive income is any source of income derived from activities that don't take an active involvement, or daily effort, for its generation. These would include things like real estate rental payments, dividends from stocks, sales of info products, income from blogs, ebooks, songs or movie royalties, audiobooks, and the like. Passive income is how the rich grow their net worth, without having to exert themselves that much more. Now, passive income does require some maintenance, but it doesn't require much maintenance. It doesn't require the kind of effort needed to produce active income. You see, nearly the same amount of effort and work goes into producing a passive income stream, as it does to produce an active income stream. But instead, the passive income stream continues to produce revenues far into the future, without a lot of additional effort. The active income stream dries up as soon as you quit putting effort into it. You can't make money while you sleep with an active income, but you can with a passive income.

Depending on the type of passive income stream you

decide on, you can produce revenues from one, or multiple sources. It all boils down to what you're willing to experiment with, and what your inherent skillset is. Remember the discussion about skills mastery? Well, once you've mastered a skill, whatever skill that may be, you can launch into creating a passive income stream from that. You can help to educate others about that specific skill, or use that skill to produce a product – such as a book, a blog, a song, or an educational course for instance – that will continue to pay you in passive income far after you've completed the work.

Many people looking to start out with passive incomes start small. They usually start a blog, purchase stock that pays dividend payments, or create some sort of educational course that they can sell somewhere online. Others like to dive into major endeavors such as real estate investing that produce rental income, or they write a book or a song that produces royalties, and so on. But, whatever passive income streams you decide to pursue, you have to start now. You have to start researching different types of passive incomes that you can produce in order to pay yourself on autopilot. A year from now, you'll wish you started today, and today, you probably wish you started a year ago. So, start today. There's no better time than the present. After you've tackled your financial picture, get started on passive income streams.

Now, this is easier said than done. There are people who prey on unsuspecting folks who are looking to make more money on the Internet. They promise them money and riches by signing up to their network-marketing program, or some other online program that will make them rich overnight. Don't get sucked into that. Realize that whatever you decide to start, it's going to take a long time to see results. If you decide to start a blog, it will be years of hard work before that blog begins to produce a passive income stream for you. And, even after it begins producing a passive income stream, a blog takes maintenance. You must continue to write articles for a blog and post them on a periodic basis. It's not completely hands-free.

However, many passive income streams are virtually hands free. You could write a book, if you have a specific skillset that you can professionally teach people about. But writing isn't for everyone. It takes a tremendous amount of diligent effort exerted over a very long period. Plus, results are slow with writing. But if you're looking for something fast, you must be willing to put up money to make money. By investing in things like real estate, stocks with dividends, or existing businesses with passive income streams, such as insurance brokerages, you can create passive incomes much quicker. It's not going to happen overnight. No matter what you do, you're either going to need a lot of time, or a lot of money. Since most people who are starting out in the millionaire method don't have a lot of money, you're going to have to learn to invest a lot of your time, wisely.

However, it's better to invest your time in something that will continue to pay you back, than investing it in something that will only pay you an active wage once. Now, most people simply can't afford to leave an active wage job to pursue only passive income streams, but there's nothing stopping you from working on a passive income stream in your spare time while you keep your active employment. But, this does involve an enormous amount of mental, and emotional commitment. It involves keeping the psychic apparatus in check, and really embodying the millionaire traits, because for one, it takes sincere conviction. It takes a lot of conviction to see something like that through, especially when there's nobody standing behind you, telling you what to do. Most people do much better when they have a specific set of tasks that someone else is requiring them to do. But, you must break out of that mold and take initiative.

ONLINE PASSIVE INCOME STREAMS

One of the most popular passive income streams that people like to engage in is in the creation of online passive income streams. This is because the cost to market is very low. You won't have to invest a lot of money to get an online passive income stream going. But, what you don't invest in money, you have to invest in sweat equity. Depending on how much time you have on your hands, you need to gauge just how much of it you can spare for your online endeavors. However, if you've seen or heard about people "cashing in," so to speak, on the Internet, it's true. But, it takes a lot of work on the front-end. It takes a lot of effort in setup and marketing to generate a good passive income stream online.

The single most popular way to create a passive income stream on the Internet is to start a blog. Blogging has huge upside potential, and can generate a windfall of cash, but it's not going to happen overnight. It's going to take you years of effectively writing articles for both human eyes, and for the search engines. It takes a lot of effort to get your articles to appear at the top of organic search results on Google. That's why the industry is so elusive. There are a small number of people at the very top making an enormous amount of income, then there are the others along the bottom who are frustrated and fed up. The ones at the bottom hardly produce enough money per month to pay for a single meal, while those at the top, can generate upwards of millions per year in passive income streams.

However, to get to that number of generating millions per year in passive income, your blog has to be very seasoned. Meaning that, Google has to have a history of finding your blog articles over the course of several years before it begins trusting your blog enough to show your results at the top of its search engine results pages. And, even after years of writing, if those blog articles don't provide an enormous amount of value to readers, then you're wasting your time. That's how Google looks at it, and rightfully so. If you don't provide a lot of value to people, then Google doesn't want to give you a top-ranking search result. Its aim is for high-quality results that provide a lot of value, because that's what its users are looking for.

Just think of it yourself. When you're searching for something on Google, you want to find the most relevant search results with the best information, at the top. That's because you're most likely going to click one of those top listings. You're not going to want to sift through and search endlessly to find what you're looking for. Google knows that people are impatient. It knows that people are looking for information, and they want it fast, so it has to provide them with the best information at the top. That's why the field of blogging is so competitive. There's huge upside at the top to earn money, but a lot of competition. Naturally, when there's huge upside potential for profit in something, the masses are attracted. But, when most people realize the enormous amount of work blogging takes, they usually stop dead in their tracks.

This is where the millionaire traits of honesty, skills mastery, communication, conviction, and adaptability come into play. You require all of these to engage in a successful blogging career. For example, if you employ dishonest tactics, and try to do things like sneaky redirects to push Website visitors to unintended pages, Google will penalize you. Blogging also takes excellent communication skills. You want to be able to convey the message in your blog articles, to the best of your ability. When you do this, and you provide a lot of value, people take notice. When people take notice, they bookmark your blog, and continue to come back, but this also makes Google take notice as well, thus moving you up in the search rankings. But, blogging also takes conviction. You have to be truly committed to blogging, and you can't just give up right away. It takes the conviction to continue writing blogs week after week, even while earning little to no income from your efforts. And, of course, blogging takes adaptability. You have to be able to adapt to changes that occur in search engine algorithms for example, or changing tides for the type and style of information people are looking for.

But, if you're committed to starting a blogging career, setting one up isn't a huge amount of effort. The effort is really in growing and maintaining that blog. In a book entitled *SEO for Bloggers – Learn How to Rank your Blog Posts at the Top of Google's Search Results,* I discuss just what it takes to effectively setup a blog and optimize it for Google's search results. The entire purpose of the book is to help people climb Google's search rankings, and help to demystify some of the knowledge in the very obscure industry of SEO. If you're committed to blogging, and creating a passive income stream from you blog, then you need to understand things like SEO, and you need to understand them intrinsically.

Network Marketing

Another type of passive income stream that you can create online involves network marketing. Sometimes, people refer to this as affiliate marketing, and depending upon how you feel about being an aggressive sales person in this capacity, it may or may not be for you. In network marketing, you can generate commissions from your own direct sales, but also from the sales persons that you affiliate yourself with. These are the sales persons that you yourself brought on board, and they act as affiliates within your own network.

But it's important to know that many network-marketing companies on the Internet have gotten a bad wrap because of their sales tactics. The way that the most successful network marketers make their money is by creating a lot of hype around the product or service their company is offering. What they don't convey well to the end user is just how much work is going to be involved in building an email list, and growing your downline (the members and affiliates who sign up beneath you). And, there's the fact that some of these network-marketing companies are thinly-veiled pyramid schemes, which only really serve those on top, which is why the FTC is cracking down on them so hard. So, it's important that you know all the risks and downsides involved before you get involved in something like this. However, if you can be successful at network marketing or affiliate marketing, you can make an enormous passive income stream. You just have to ask yourself whether you really want to do something like that in the little time that you do have to spare.

Photography

If you're creatively inclined, you could take up the field

of photography, for example, and generate a passive income by taking photos in your spare time. By shooting professional images, and uploading them to stock photography Websites like Shutterstock.com for example, or iStockPhoto.com, you can generate a passive income anytime they license or sell your photos. And while photography isn't for everyone, it certainly is something that carries a bit more pride in it than other online income generating opportunities involving network marketing. You can feel proud that you're providing a huge amount of value in return for passive income, especially when your photography is very good.

And, photography is something that many people can do; it's not just something for professionals. The great thing about the Internet is that it opens the doors to average people who can utilize its very many avenues to help improve their own financial situation. However, just like anything else, photography takes work. It takes work to look at your subject from a creative mind, and play around with photo editing software. It takes work, just as everything else takes work, but if you're going to dive into something, then pick a field and do it. Don't give up. Don't allow your ego to push you back towards your emotion-numbing behavior just because it doesn't want to go up against a little bit of failure. Don't allow that to happen to you.

Moreover, most good phones these days, can take very high-quality photos, and some even have photo-editing software apps that are inexpensive to purchase. Of course, a phone is a small area to work off for photography, so you might want to use your laptop and have a good camera. None of these things comes cheap. This too, is another avenue that can pay off well down the road long after the work is complete. It can generate a passive income stream for you that will keep going and going, long after you've shot and edited those photos.

eBook Publishing

If you have a passion for writing, you could try your hand at publishing eBooks. The art of eBook publishing has exploded to the masses, but it's important to note that, it's difficult to succeed in eBook sales. Just like anything else worthwhile, it takes a tremendous amount of work and effort. However, the satisfaction of writing and publishing your work to the world is unlike any other out there. And, you can generate a passive income that will pay you back long after the work has been completed. If you're not afraid to get your hands dirty, and are willing to put in the long and grueling hours required of an author, then this is an excellent way to generate some passive income.

Once you've created your books, you can also generate them into print-on-demand paperbacks, and audiobooks as well. There are several different mediums for publishing eBooks today, the most popular of which are Amazon (available at kdp.amazon.com), Nook.com, Kobo.com, Smashwords.com, and Lulu.com. If you want to try your hand at print-on-demand paperbacks, you can publish those same digital works at Createspace.com. If you're inclined to produce audiobooks, you can use ACX.com, which will feed your audiobooks into iTunes, Audible.com, and Amazon.com. Whichever you decide to do, pick an avenue for publishing, and commit yourself to finishing that book, no matter what. And, remember that the author's work doesn't finish after you publish, because there's the long and grueling road of marketing your work as well.

9

MULTIPLE STREAMS OF DIVERSE REVENUE

"Being good in business is the most fascinating art. Making money is art and working is art and good business is the best art." – Andy Warhol

We've seen some examples of passive income streams, but we all know how difficult passive income is to generate. You either need a lot of time, or a lot of money to get started. But, passive income is important, and this should always be something you're working on in the background. But, you must also devote your time and your energy to generating multiple streams of diverse revenue. Aside from your day job, and your passive income endeavors, there are multiple streams of diverse revenue you can generate both online and offline. The goal here is to have as many sources of income as possible so that you're not solely reliant on only one to support you. And, if one of them should happen to fizzle out and die on you, you have others to support you.

Creating multiple streams of diverse revenue is also one of the prerequisites to leaving your day job. While a day job working for someone else can pay the bills, it won't afford you the opportunity for untethering the financial cord. It won't allow you to fulfill your dream of becoming financially free, because it's going to drain the one precious resource we all have in common, and that's time. Since we all have an equal amount of time, we have to use it wisely. There's only a certain amount of time in the day, and no matter who you are, or where you live, we all have the same amount of time on our hands.

When it comes to active streams of revenue that you can engage in, part-time or full-time on the Web, you can choose from many. Depending on your area of expertise, there are hundreds of legitimate money making opportunities on the Web. The best thing about working online, is that you can literally be anywhere in the world you choose to be. And, when you're able to actively increase your passive income stream, while also increasing your secondary active income streams, you can be on the road to untethering that financial cord from your nine-to-five job. That is, if you work for someone else.

If you currently work for yourself, then a congratulations is in order. You are one of the very many brave souls in the world who have ventured out there to try their hand at entrepreneurship. But, as you may have already found out, working for yourself can be difficult. Like everything else that has to do with income streams, having the discipline to work when no one else is pushing you to do so, can be extremely difficult at times. Making enough to survive is one thing, but being able to make enough money to thrive is an entirely different thing. And, working for yourself can get especially frustrated when you either have a lack of money, lack of new business, or not enough time to complete your work. Time management is an invaluable skill to the entrepreneur, and the better you can manage your time, the more effective you'll be with the millionaire method.

When it comes to active revenue streams, there are many different activities that you can engage in on the Web to "cash in," so-to-speak. All from the comfort of your own home, you can generate money by participating in several different online services that bring together service providers with buyers. Some of the largest online marketplaces allow entrepreneurs to entirely supplement their full-time job's income, all from the comfort of their own home. But, again, this boils down to skillset, and if you don't have a particular skill, it doesn't hurt to develop it as you build your business. Just remember to play by the millionaire method's rules and embody the traits. As long as you stick to the rules and embody the traits, even if you're running your own business from home, you will eventually get ahead. Remember, slow and steady will win the race. Don't think of this as a sprint, but rather a marathon.

STARTING YOUR OWN ONLINE BUSINESS

One of the best ways to make money online is to start your own business. For many budding entrepreneurs, this is the quickest way to leaving their nine-to-five job, but it isn't necessarily the quickest route to financial freedom. Starting your own online business, while very satisfying, takes a lot of work. You essentially become your own marketing department, sales department, customer service department, human resources department, and accounting department. With so many hats to wear, juggling all of the tasks required for entrepreneurs can be overwhelming. Still, if you're ready to strike out on your own, the Internet is the best place to start.

No matter what your skillset is, you can create an additional stream of revenue for yourself by marketing your skills on the Internet. You can even start without setting up your own Website – for those of you who are frightened by the very thought of doing that – by using one of the many different online services on the Web. By tapping into Websites like elance.com, guru.com, and freelancer.com, you can market a whole slew of services. And, depending on what you're marketing, and how well your presentation is, you can do extremely well online. Some of the more popular types of services to offer through sites like these are:

- Graphic or Web design

- Virtual assistant

- Customer or client services

- Accounting services

- Tutoring or educational services

- Ghostwriting and blogging services

- Business consulting services

- Resume writing services

- Career or headhunting services

Of course, these are just the ones you can do from the comfort of your own home, there are of course loads more that you can do away you're your home. And, if you're trying to market in-person services, you can sell or market just about any kind of service by using Websites like craigslist.com, fiverr.com, and backpages.com. Here is a list of services you can market through Websites like that, but please ensure that you research the proper licensing requirements for providing any of these services. It's your duty to ensure that you protect yourself when you go into business for yourself.

- Home child daycare

- Personal shopping services

- Yoga or personal training

- Tutoring for musical instruments

- Tutoring for languages

- Tutoring for school courses

- Answering or assistant services

- Elderly care

- CPA and tax services

- Paralegal and legal services

- Home improvement services"

- Cooking or personal chef services

- Home or office organization

- Home appliance installation and repair

Whatever you decide to do, the important thing is to just do it. Procrastination is the silent killer, and if you sit around for too long and second-guess yourself, you'll never make progress. Just think about how good it will feel when you can run your own successful business from the comfort of your home. Just imagine how much better you will feel when you open your eyes in the morning. It's not going to be easy; none of it will. Whether you start your own business, or you engage in some other passive or active income generating activities, it's going to take a lot of hard work. But, think about the alternative. Think about slaving away while lining someone else's pockets for the rest of your life. How does that make you feel? How would it feel if you were to lose your job and be without a primary income stream? If it's happened to you, as it has to millions of others, you know it doesn't feel good. It never feels good.

Striking out on your own, and starting up your own business involves a lot of planning. Aside from deciding on a corporate and legal structure, you have your tax planning, general accounting, marketing, sales, and other operational concerns. It's enough to keep you up at night, especially when the sales aren't coming in. But, you have to understand that anything worthwhile is going to be hard. Anything that you try to set out to do in order to generate money online, or offline, will be hard. Even if you fall victim to one of those late night infomercials that offer you the miracle at-home system for making money, they will be hard unless you do the work. If you're not a stranger to doing hard work, then any of those systems will eventually generate income, it's just a matter of how tenacious you are. It depends on how long you can last, and how long you can hang in there. If you throw in the towel early, nothing is going to work. Nothing will ever work if you just decide to quit and start something new all the time. You have to pick something and stick to it. It's both as difficult and as simple as that.

OTHER REVENUE SOURCES

I wanted to put together another resource of listings that you can utilize to make money on the Internet, aside from just starting your own business. Some of these require capital, while others don't, but they are all worth checking out and doing the due diligence for them. Remember to always do your homework, no matter what you get yourself involved in. Always go in and research things before jumping in headfirst. Talk to the proper people to help assess the best moves for your own situation. A small amount of money invested now in legal and tax planning, will pay off enormously later on. Follow the millionaire method's rules always.

Crowd-Sourced Lending

One good revenue stream that you can jump into with a fair amount of ease, is crowd-sourced lending. There are literally hundreds of sites dedicated to helping entrepreneurs looking for loans to start their own businesses, or to receive personal loans. You can either be on the receiving end, or the giving end. When you're on the giving end, you can make a nice interest rate, which beats leaving your money to sit in the bank. You can also decide whom you want to lend your money to based on their credit score and business type, amongst a variety of other factors. Websites like prosper.com, and lendingclub.com allow you to lend and receive loans. Please note that these Websites are for US residents. If you're a resident of the UK, you can check out a Website like zopa.com, or communitylend.com if you're a resident of Canada.

Aside from those specific Websites, you can do a few simple searches on the Web to find other crowd-sourced lending, and micro-lending Websites. You can make your money back, plus some interest. It's a great way to make your money work for you, aside from just leaving it to sit in the bank and collect dust. But, be sure that you're only investing your disposable income (or your income after taxes), to avoid getting yourself into a situation where you're in a panic because you don't have the money to pay your taxes because you invested it all. Be smart, plan, and meet with your tax professional, and legal professional, before deciding on any investment like this.

Affiliate Marketing

While it has its passive income characteristics, affiliate marketing takes a sincere effort in active marketing, and promotion, in order to see it truly work. But, in order to be successful in affiliate marketing, you have to be able to drive traffic, and to be able to drive traffic, you need your own Website or blog. Without a blog, and the ability to write fresh content on a periodic basis, you'll really have no way of drawing in visitors with the hopes of landing a sale. And, not only do you need a blog with a lot of traffic, the traffic has to be targeted traffic as well.

For example, since you can sell just about any product you want through an affiliate relationship with online stores such as Amazon.com, and others, the blogs themselves must contain targeted links to the products in your cross-promotional efforts. You can't have a Website dedicated to tech gadgets, and expect to sell housewares. And, although this may sound like common sense, and easy enough to accomplish, it truly is a difficult feat to pull off. It's difficult to have the discipline to constantly blog and drive a lot of traffic to your Website. It's very difficult. However, if you can manage to do so, over the years, your ability to sell products through affiliate marketing will grow tremendously.

There are three major sources for affiliate marketing of products online. The most popular that exist today are from the major players in the market. The three are as follows:

- **Amazon Associates** – You can use the Amazon Associates Website to market and sell just about anything offered by Amazon. Since Amazon is the largest online retailer in the world, it goes without saying that they should have products to fit just about any blog or Website category that you can think of.

- **Clickbank** – Clickbank is a Website that has been around since 1998, and they offer an incredible resource for products that you can market as an affiliate. There's a wide range of products here from e-books, to online software, and everything in between. There's something to fit just about every single niche possible.

- **Commission Junction** – This Website houses affiliate marketing for some of the most well known companies in the world. You can sign up, and start earning affiliate commissions immediately for products and services that most people are already purchasing. The trick behind this of course is having enough Web traffic to be able to get people clicking your links and making sales.

Email Marketing

Some people think that email marketing is dead, but it's alive and ticking with a vengeance. Email marketing is the strategy used by some of the top network marketers, and affiliate marketers in the world, to sell products and services. But, the most difficult part of email marketing is building your list. To be an effective email marketer, you have to build a list with thousands of subscribers who want to receive the type of information that you're offering in your emails. For example, if you're trying to sell people on weight loss products, you'll want a list of people who've expressed an interest in that in the past.

But, like anything else, building your list can take years. There are ways to quicken the pace by purchasing lists from other people, but depending on the quality of those lists, you may or may not be getting the best email addresses. The best way to build a list is on your own, over time, by having a subscription box located on your Website. You can integrate that subscription box into any of the popular email systems out there today such as aweber.com, constantcontact.com, or getresponse.com. There are many more out there, but those are the most popular ones. You will also have to get very good at creating emails to those subscribers that don't sound too salesy or spammy, or risk getting flagged and reported.

Product Marketing

Another category of selling that you could do online would be to sell your own products. Of course, this entails a much more active involvement in the income stream since you'll not only be responsible for making the products, but also for shipping them, and providing customer service as well. Whether you make arts and crafts, personalized jewelry, knitted sweaters, or anything in between, you can leverage several online resources to sell those wares. Of course, you may also have a supplier that you're able to source some inexpensive products from such as iPhone cases, and resell them yourself by adding your own personal touch to them. Just remember to think creatively, and you'll be able to come up with something.

These Websites will not only provide you with an easy-to-use system for uploading products with photos, adding descriptions, and so on, but they will also facilitate the sale through their own ecommerce software built-in to their Websites. If you have products that you've been itching to sell on the Web, or have a supplier to source an inexpensive product in bulk that you know has high demand and will sell on the Web, then you should look into using Websites like Ebay.com, Etsy.com, Custommade.com, or Sellz.com. Sellz.com will only provide you with an ecommerce system, but you'll need to do the promoting through your own avenues such as through social media, Craigslist.com, or through email.

The others all have their own large customer bases, which include the selling platform as well, providing a very inexpensive cost to market with enormous visibility for your products.

Room Rentals & Vacation Rentals

Another stream of income you could generate would be to rent out a room in your house as either a short-term rental or a long-term rental. Now, if you're already renting, you may not be able to get away with this. However, some landlords don't mind since the room rentals occur while the tenants are still occupying the home. If you're renting, you should check all local, city, and state regulations where you live, along with checking to see if your landlord approves. However, this can be an excellent source of additional revenue for you.

If you're looking to just rent out a room in your house, you could use a Website like airbnb.com to post your listing. They take a small commission from the rentals, and it doesn't cost anything to list your home; you only pay the commission when a rental occurs. You could also consider renting out your entire house if you're the owner. Short-term vacation rental incomes, in some markets, can be as much as five to nine times more income potential than long-term rentals. If you own a home in a highly sought after vacation area, then this is something to consider, especially if you're looking at purchasing a second home. Look into Websites like vrbo.com, homeaway.com, and vacationrentals.com, but note that they charge high fees to list your property. You can also market any of these types of rentals on craigslist.com, or backpages.com.

10

NECESSITY IS THE MOTHER OF INVENTION

"Ability is what you're capable of doing. Motivation determines what you do. Attitude determines how well you do it." – Raymond Chandler

On this earth, there are many people dreaming of the good life. Many people claim they want to live a better life, but when it comes down to it, they fall into the wealth traps, and are stifled by their own psychic apparatuses. They are caught up in so many of the pitfalls of their own personal psychology that drives them to make mistakes, and leads them to financial ruin. And, when left unchecked, these mistakes compound upon one another, making it harder, and harder to extricate one's self from the pile of dung created in the wake of these constant mistakes.

The biggest difference between the talkers, and the doers, is that the latter make success a must. It goes from a _should_ to a _must_. The talkers know they "should" do something, while the doers know that they "must" do something. When you must do something, it becomes a necessity. Everything else standing in your way becomes small obstacles that are easy to tackle, because you constantly have your eye on the prize. You're constantly aware of the direction that you want to travel in. But, when it's a "should," you become more lackadaisical. Why do you think some of the most successful people can oftentimes come from such humble beginnings? Growing up, they were ingrained with the fact that they must succeed if they wanted a better life; it was never an option for them.

When you can envision something so powerfully in your mind, and make it a necessity, all it takes is some action to fuel that fire of achievement. Eventually, over time, you will succeed. And, as you've seen with the many ways that are required to be successful, none of it happens overnight. Even if you were to win the lottery tomorrow, statistics say that 70% of those people go broke. If you don't truly appreciate how money works, and earn it from the ground up, it's easy to get caught up in the inner wrangling of your psychic apparatus, and allow money to slip right through your hands. It's easy for your id and your ego to control you when it comes to money, and it's oftentimes hard to let the superego to suppress those urges. Be aware of this and conscious of it at all times.

The most important thing that you have to keep in mind is to create an action plan for yourself. Make success a necessity, and create a plan of action, detailing out the steps that you're going to take to achieve success. And, you can even work backwards. Start with the amount of money you wish to possess, whether it's one million, ten million, one hundred million, and so on, and work backwards. But, set realistic goals. If you've never made more than one hundred thousand dollars, euros, pounds, or the equivalent in a year, don't say you'll make a hundred million in twelve months. Be realistic, setup a five-year plan, and work backwards. What are you going to do to achieve that success? How are you going to eliminate your debt and setup additional sources of revenue?

You have to become like a detective, and success is the crime that you're researching. Look to others in fields similar to yours. What did they do to become successful? What sacrifices did they make? Anything worthwhile is going to take hard work, so dig in your heels, and grind. Time is going to pass by quickly anyhow, so wouldn't you rather you were doing something productive with it? Promise yourself one year of commitment to your goals, and see just how much you can accomplish. You'll be surprised at what you can pull off in the matter of a year. You can accomplish so much in year that no matter what your present situation, you can truly turn it around and accomplish just about anything.

Getting Started

The hardest part about becoming successful is merely getting started. It's hard to decide to act, and just do it. Life can be stifling at times, and we would all rather slip back into the emotion-numbing activities that our psychic apparatus wants to keep us in. But, you have to break that pattern. You have to disrupt your way of thinking by building awareness at what's going on. You have to realize that it's going to be more pain, not more pleasure, if you don't deal with matters now. You must come to that realization, because otherwise, the ego and the id will continue to try to get their way.

But, once you do get started, building momentum becomes easier and easier, as time goes on. As the days, weeks, months, and years slip by, you'll notice you're self-compounding on your successes, little by little. With each passing moment, you will become more empowered to push through your present-day limitations, and break through those fears and those anxieties that have been holding you back. However, you have to paint that financial picture for yourself. You have to truly look at your situation, and the status of your affairs. You have to be completely honest and forthright with yourself. By lying to yourself, you're only hurting your own chances for success. The ego pushes us to that point. The ego tries to mask and protect us from the pain, so it allows the id to win. The id takes over, and begins to run and ruin our lives.

If an activity or behavior you knew was bad for you sucked you in, and you did it anyways, you allowed the id to run your life. You allowed that pleasure-driven part of your psychic apparatus to take hold, and not let go. The problem is that, most people don't know how to moderate. When they are sucked into a behavior, it begins to take control of their lives, and it leads to a slow and eventual demise. But, it's also so difficult to see your own problems. That's usually why it takes people several times of severe failure until they can recognize their own limiting behaviors. It takes truly hitting an emotional rock bottom before you can force yourself forward.

Don't allow yourself to hit an emotional and financial rock bottom that is going to take years to dig out of. If you take control of the reigns, you can fix it now, as long as you get started now. There's no excuses for putting off tomorrow, what can be done today. If you know deep down inside that you should do something, then do it. Look at your life from the perspective of an outsider looking in. Try to recognize the flaws that exist and work to correct them. Don't allow your ego to run your life, because it has a tendency to do that. No matter who you are, it can control you, if you don't do something to stop it.

Furthermore, starting now isn't hard. You can do something, no matter how small it is, towards the attainment of your financial goals. Write a short list for yourself of what you want to achieve. Do you want to start a business? Great! What can you do right now to get that business off the ground? Well, you could brainstorm types of businesses that you can start. Spend 15 minutes with a piece of paper writing out just what you think you can sell. Is it a product? Is it a service? Think about it. And, where will you sell it? This brainstorming is the first step in creating that thought, which can so easily come to life over time. It's all in the mind.

And, if you're trying to get out of debt, then that should be your primary focus. Remember the financial picture that you painted for yourself in the earlier chapter? Great, now what can you do to extricate yourself from that? Where can you cut the spending? Did you actually do the work to lay things out on paper to see where you stand? If you didn't do it, go back and do it. The financial picture that you paint for yourself is the most important step for battling your own psychic apparatus. It's important because the ego won't have a place to hide when you unveil the truth about your financial situation. You can't expect to continue on the same path with any better results if you don't do the work.

The truth is that without short-term pain, you can't have long-term gain. No matter what area of our lives we're talking about, short-term pain is a precursor to long-term gain. Think about it. Whether you're trying to do weight loss, get out of debt, or achieve any other goal, short-term pain will always precede the long-term gain.

The short-term pain exists because we're normally so set in our stubborn patterns and ways of life. We're creatures of comfort that are so used to doing things one way, that it's hard for us to see any other way of doing them. But, the important thing is to recognize this, and work to correct it. Understand that it's just how you are, and it's something that's built into you, from years and years of conditioning. It's not something to be afraid of or embarrassed about. Everyone goes through rough patches in life. It happens to all of us.

When you encounter fear and anxiety, it's just the ego trying to protect your fragile inner self. It's trying to protect you from the potential hurt and pain that you may suffer at the hands of others. But, the ego is what is helping to protect us amongst our peers, and across the relationships that we have. The ego is trying to preserve whatever sense of self or identification we've created amongst our own network of friends and family. The ego works to help protect us from the critics, because if we were to exist alone on this earth, there wouldn't be anyone to criticize us or act negatively towards us. But, you have to realize that's just the way people are. People will always talk. There's nothing to ever be embarrassed about. Unless what you know you're doing is wrong, be confident in your actions and be steadfast.

As soon as you allow others to have that kind of control over you, you're doomed. You're doomed because, once the ego takes hold in this respect, it doesn't let go. It pushes you further and further into a spiral, spinning you completely out of control. You begin to lose every sense of your self while only trying to keep up appearances. It becomes a vicious cycle that people repeat over, and over again, with no end in sight. It's the root cause for why we have so many financial meltdowns in our economies. People spend more than they make, and they break the cardinal rules of the millionaire method. If you can realize this, and learn to play by the rules, you'll slowly make progress. But, unlike the pleasure-seeking id's desires for instant gratification, it won't happen overnight.

Succeeding in life involves toiling. Sometimes it involves seemingly endless toiling. Most people search and search, try and try again, and keep hitting roadblocks along the way. And this will happen to you too. Pushing through those limitations are difficult, that's why so few people achieve success; that's why so few people embody the millionaire method. Most people would rather take the time to go out and do something fun, spend their money, and forget about their problems. We tend to indulge in this escapist behavior in order to further shroud ourselves from the real truth. We don't want to open our eyes and see what's before us. We don't want to open our ears to truly hear what's going on. It's painful, and rightfully so. It's going to be painful.

SEEK AND YOUR SHALL FIND

The mind has a funny way of helping you to find the answers to your problems, when you look at your problems in an honest fashion. When you don't ignore what's happening all around you, the mind has this way of helping you resolve those problems. That's because, so much is going on in the background of your thinking, without you even knowing about it. So much mental juggling is happening, that you couldn't even begin to fathom it. In those 50,000 or so thoughts you have each day, your mind is constantly weighing and calculating the cause and effect of things. But, the problem is, most of that is occurring in your subconscious mind. You're not aware of most of the thoughts running through your head.

Remember that thoughts are things, and what you focus on, you will manifest in your life. The truth of the matter is that most people focus on the negative, so they manifest more negativity. It doesn't mean you should ignore your problems, it means you should recognize them in an honest fashion, and then do what you have to do in order to resolve them, but be positive. Focus on the good that a situation will bring rather than the bad. Focus on how you will grow and become a better person because of all of this. Because, we are all here to grow and contribute something of our selves to this world, and through experiences, we do that. When you begin to seek different ways you can generate more income or get out of debt, your mind will eventually help you find the way. The mind is extremely powerful in that aspect.

What you have in your life right now is a direct reflection of your thoughts and your focus. Whether those are good things or bad things, you manifested them. You held onto a certain thought, which brought that thing into existence in your life. What you must do is be honest about what you have and what you've manifested in your life. If those have been bad things, then you have to learn to change your focus. Don't focus on the bad things, people, or events of your life. You have to think positive. And, if those things, people, or events weigh you down, and you can change your situation, then change it. Don't be a creature of comfort; don't fall into habit and routine. Make some changes.

Opening your eyes to the world is hard. It's hard to take a good look at what's going on, and to have an honest perspective of your own situation. But you must do it. Open your eyes and look. Open your ears and hear. When you can do this, you can truly grow. You can learn to overcome any obstacle that you put your mind to. It's the truth of the matter. No matter what you focus on, you will manifest. Think about the world for a moment, and how much of it all used to be a thought. If you were to travel back in time, and tell someone 100 years ago that we would have electric cars, and spaceships gearing up for commercial space travel, they would have laughed at you. If you were to tell them about the speed and efficiency of modern day communications because of telecom and the Web, they would have thought you were crazy.

One hundred years ago, those were just dreams at best. They were science fiction. And, what we dream of today, will eventually become reality. As outlandish as something may seem to you, or as ridiculous as your goals may sound, in the long term, anything is possible. You can achieve and do anything that you set your mind to. It's just a matter of how much conviction and motivation you have to achieve those goals. If you set out to do something, and you put your mind to it, you can accomplish anything. All of us can. It doesn't take a special person to achieve great things; it just takes a special determination. When you have determination raring in your heart like a blazing fire, nothing can stop you. Nothing can slow down the determined man or woman who sets their mind to accomplishing something, literally nothing.

11

ACTIONS SPEAK LOUDER THAN WORDS

"Action speaks louder than words, but not nearly as often." – Mark Twain

Actions speak louder than words. We've all heard that saying, and when it comes to your finances, it couldn't be more important. Your actions speak louder than words, because we all say we want to do something about our finances, but we mostly don't do it. Why is that? Why do we allow things to get so bad, before they can get better? Why do most people have to reach a financial rock bottom, before they can begin picking up the pieces? Well, what happens when you hit the bottom is that you're forced to take a good, hard, and honest look at the picture. You're forced to look at all of your debt, see where your expenses are going each month, and find out how you can fix the big mess.

But it doesn't have to take financial ruin for you to get on track. Actions speak louder than words, because if you truly want something, then you must take action towards the attainment of it. If you want to get out of debt, paint your financial picture. Painstakingly go through every last red cent you owe, and find out your true net worth. Are you in a deep and dark hole of never-ending debt? If you are, then the more pain you present to the ego, the better. The more pain you can inflict on it, the more you will have a chance to subdue the id, and allow the superego to reign supreme. You have to be brutally honest with yourself. You have to be brutally honest about your present situation and just how you got there. It doesn't take rocket science, just an honest approach.

But actions speak louder than words means more than just that. It means more than just climbing out of debt. It means true financial freedom. Just imagine how good it would feel to open your eyes in the morning and not have to answer anyone. Just imagine how good it would feel to open your eyes and not have to clamor to get ready for a job that you can't stand doing. Can you imagine how good that would feel? If you're picturing it in your mind, I bet it feels good. I bet you can just see it vividly. But, if that's not your scenario today, why isn't it? Why are you not financially free? Remember, actions speak louder than words, so do something about it. Make a plan and do something.

The hardest part of untethering the financial cord is getting started. Since we do more to avoid pain than gain pleasure, it's difficult to push towards something that may be years out down the road, when we have today's financial pressures pushing in on us. But, you must do something today. One year from now, you'll wish you started today. Just imagine how much you can accomplish in one year. Even if it takes you endless nights with little to no sleep to create the life of your dreams, isn't it worth it?

But, we all know what happens. We get stuck in those bad behaviors. We are creatures of comfort and of habit, and we easily slip back into patterns that foster negativity for us.

The hardest part is getting started. The hardest part is deciding today – right now – to do something about it. The hardest part is making that decision that can singlehandedly change the course of your life. This isn't about getting rich quick; it's about slowly pushing towards financial freedom. It won't happen overnight, and you can't expect that instant gratification, otherwise you'll just get frustrated. You'll get more, and more frustrated, especially if you try to buy into programs that tout their ability to make you rich overnight. They generally don't work, especially if you don't work them. If you work a get-rich-quick scheme, you might be successful, but it won't happen quickly. It will happen after a very long and arduous path of pushing and pushing.

BEATING PROCRASTINATION

One thing that stifles action is procrastination; it's the silent killer. Procrastination can stop you dead in your tracks, in whatever goal you may be pursuing. When it comes to your finances, throwing a blind eye to what's before you only leads to more procrastination. When the ego shrouds the truth from you, it helps to foster this air of procrastination that allows you to slip back into your emotion-numbing behavior. If you knew the truth, and understood the severity of the pain that was ahead of you, you couldn't slip into procrastination; you would have to do something about it. The ego knows this, and it uses this as one of its subconscious tools for shrouding the truth from you.

In any kind of action in life, procrastination can destroy your pursuit of a goal. No matter what you're striving towards, don't allow procrastination to stifle you. Don't allow the power of this force to overcome you and take hold. Because, when it does, breaking the patterns and habits become extraordinarily difficult. Make a plan, and do something towards the attainment of that plan. Do a little bit each day, and you'll eventually move closer, and closer to your goal. But, don't allow yourself to just sit on the sidelines with an air of indifference. Don't allow yourself to get comfortable in your pleasure-driven pursuits that eventually will lead to a much more painful situation.

If you've had difficulty with procrastination in the past, look at your situation with honesty. This doesn't just apply to your financial picture; this applies to any goal in life. Whatever you're looking to accomplish, as long as you can be honest with yourself enough to realize that there's more pain by not doing something, than there is in putting it off any longer, you'll have to do something. You'll have to do something because if you don't, things are going to get a lot worse.

But, it's also important that your goals mean something to you. If your goal is to be financially free, and you're looking to break a pattern of procrastination, how important is untethering the financial cord? What does it actually mean to you? When you have a strong enough meaning behind why you want to do something, you can achieve it. Think back to the past when you had a goal and you achieved it. You had a strong burning desire, a passion deep down inside, which meant something to you. You attributed a strong enough meaning and reason as to why you wanted to achieve your goal. Because you did that, you were able to overcome all of the obstacles that were in your way.

When you want something bad enough, you'll go out there and do whatever it takes to achieve it. You'll go out there and work tirelessly to achieve that goal. However, when what you're after doesn't mean that much to you, you won't work so hard. You won't have sleepless nights and never-ending days. It won't be that important to you. But, as soon as the meaning is important enough, and you have a strong enough reason, you'll overcome anything to achieve that goal. For example, if you just want to be financially free only to have more money to spend, that's not a good enough meaning. There isn't a good enough reason behind that goal. But, if you want to be financially free, because you want your children to live a good life, and not have to suffer the way that you did, then that's a stronger meaning. And, since most of us do more for others than we do for ourselves, setting your goals that are attributed to your family is a good start for your quest in financial freedom.

Each person has to have their own unique set of reasons and meanings behind their goals; it has to be a passionate pursuit for you otherwise, you won't follow through. It has to be a burning desire in your heart that will make you climb the tallest mountain, and swim the widest ocean. Can you see the difference here? Find a strong enough meaning and reason for why you want financial freedom, and each day remind yourself of that, and eventually you'll achieve it. Eventually you'll achieve all of your goals of financial freedom. It's inevitable.

OTHER BOOKS IN THIS SERIES

Thank you for taking the time to read this book. I truly hope that you enjoyed it, and I would like to take a moment of your time to share your thoughts with the online community by posting a review on Amazon. If this book inspired you in any way, shape, or form, I would love to hear about it in a book review. You can find the Amazon Book page located at the following URL - http://www.amazon.com/dp/B00DXLAEG8

I put a lot of care into the books that I write and I hope that this care and sincerity come across in my writing because in the end I write to bring value to other people's lives. I hope that this book has brought some value to your life. I truly do.

This book is the seventh book in the *Inspirational Books Series* of personal development books that I've released. You can check out the other books in the series that are available as well, in the proceeding list:

R.L. ADAMS

- *How Not to Give Up* – *A Motivational &
  Inspirational Guide to Goal Setting & Achieving your
  Dreams (Volume 1)*

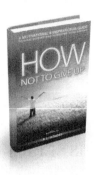

- *The Silk Merchant* – *Ancient Words of Wisdom to
  Help you Live a Better Life Today (Volume 2)*

- *Have a Little Hope* – *An Inspirational Guide to
  Discovering What Hope is and How to Have More of it in
  Your Life (Volume 3)*

- <u>*Breakthrough*</u> – *Live an Inspired Life, Overcome your Obstacles, and Accomplish your Dreams*

- <u>*How to Be Happy*</u> – *An Inspirational Guide to Discovering What Happiness is and How to have More of it in your Life*

- <u>***Move Mountains***</u> – *How to Achieve Anything in your Life with the Power of Positive Thinking (Volume 6)*

Made in the USA
Middletown, DE
16 February 2023

25032255R00126